CW00802031

On the Road to Auroville

A Spiritual Misadventure

———

Jon Stein

Fairway Publishing

First published in Great Britain in 2012 by
Fairway Publishing, Totnes, Devon
An imprint of Upfront Publishing, Peterborough.

ISBN: 978-178035-476-7

Layout and design by Strawberry Design, Totnes
www.strawberry-design.co.uk

Printed by printondemand-worldwide.com

www.jonstein.co.uk

For my Father

Contents

My Journey

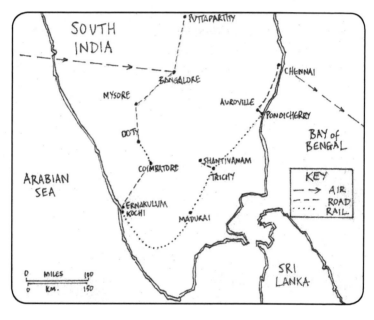

December 2008 to April 2009

Author's Note

This book, though substantially based on real events, includes elements of fiction. I have preserved the real names of most of the central characters and hope they will forgive the occasional embellishment.

My comments on, and experiences of, the various practices and treatments described in the story should not be taken too seriously!

Neither the journey, nor this book, would have been possible to undertake without the support of my family and friends. I also want to thank the many people who showed me kindness in India.

I received advice and encouragement in the writing process from Melissa Merrington-Pink, Carmella B'Hahn, Lee Cooper, Michael Elsmere, Martin Foster and Mark Leahy. Paul Beaumont gave me invaluable help with the cover.

Prologue

"Experience is what you get when you didn't get what you wanted."

Randy Pausch

'But why India?'

Down the telephone, I could hear my father frowning. It was the winter of 2008, and the recent terrorist bombings in Mumbai were fresh in both our minds. I mumbled something about going somewhere I'd always dreamed of seeing. Dad didn't seem convinced, but he was happier when I said I'd come and visit him just before leaving.

Earlier that year I had turned forty. I stood at a crossroads in my life. What did I want to do? What could I do? Chronic Fatigue Syndrome (M.E.) had cast a long, dark shadow over my thirties, and my career as a musician had for some time been limping along without much energy or enthusiasm. I had moved to the country town of Totnes to pursue a more healthy, alternative lifestyle and to be closer to the man I loved. But the relationship had foundered and my heart had shut down.

I needed a change. I needed *to* change. I'd got into Buddhism, and that seemed to be helping, but I was still running low on compassion – for others, and for myself. When a friend advised going somewhere to do some volunteering, India came to mind. Initially, I'd wanted to visit the holy Buddhist sites of the north, but friends who knew the country told me that southern India would make a gentler landing. An established ashram, they said, could provide the structure and security I needed.

So I had read up a little about Sai Baba – one of the most famous, and controversial, Indian gurus – and was intrigued by the stories of his wonder-working. Could he really manifest objects out of thin air? Was he, as some claimed, the major avatar (incarnation of God) of our age? Why not go and see him and decide for myself? After that, I could travel wherever I wanted. Besides, it wasn't such a strange choice of destination. India is famed for its spirituality and I was certainly searching for something.

I arrived in Reading on a grey December afternoon. Before long, the dining table was covered with shoes, clothes and medicines. My father looked on anxiously as I tried to fit everything into my rucksack. Aside from basic equipment, I seemed to have a lot of medical stuff: iodine and chlorine tablets to treat water, rehydration salts, and a large supply of anti-malarial drugs. Surely I'd be safe with all this? Besides, I'd had umpteen vaccinations and taken out travel insurance (though I could have done with spending some more time reading the small print of the policy).

By late evening I had got everything together and went to bed excited at the thought of the trip ahead. Before switching out the bedside lamp, I flicked through my guidebook and paused over the photos. The golden sun and cerulean skies, the bright chaos of the city streets, the dazzling whites and colours of Indian clothes, the intricate carvings of statues and temples... It all looked so vibrant and alive!

The following morning was wet and miserable. As my father drove me to Heathrow, I peered out at the trees and fields – fixing these last views of England in my mind. I didn't know when I would return and I wasn't even sure I wanted to come back. I'd bought an open-ended round-the-world ticket and hoped to go on from India to Australia, to see my sister who lived in Melbourne.

I had an emotional departure from my father at the airport, running back to the lift he had just stepped into and calling out 'I love you!' as he disappeared from view. Now I was on my own.

I sat in the departure lounge recalling the preparations of the previous few weeks. It had all been a bit of a rush (I had barely managed to get a visa in time), and now I seemed to feel the weight and momentum of all that busyness catching up with me. I also realised that, apart from starting off in Bangalore, I had no idea where I was actually going. Well, it would just have to be a journey of faith.

Around me sat other travellers: chatting, snacking, fiddling with iPods, or reading. There were Indian families dressed for the summer, some vaguely hippyish Western tourists, a few businessmen and women. I sat back and closed my eyes, imagining myself dressed in flowing white clothes, meditating beside the Ganges River...

When I woke, the lounge was almost empty. In a panic, I rushed to find the right departure gate. There, the last of my fellow passengers were now queueing to board the plane. As I showed my ticket at the desk, I felt myself leaving behind the security of life in England. For the next few months I would put aside my friends and family, my home and my activities, and would cross into another world. With a little shiver of anticipation, I stepped into the plane.

A Prisoner of Sai Baba

'You! What are you doing?'

I looked up, startled, from my sketchbook. Surrounding me were three young Indian guards. They were dressed in a scruffy mix of khaki and camouflage and each was brandishing a rifle.

'Me? I'm just drawing.' I tried to keep the fear out of my voice.

We were standing in front of a shrine within Sai Baba's ashram at Puttaparthy, near Bangalore. Crowds of devotees were returning from the afternoon darshan (audience) with the guru.

The eldest looking guard flicked through my sketchpad, darting threatening looks in my direction. Aside from the half-finished view of the temple, there was also a drawing I had made that morning whilst waiting inside the accommodation office, detailing the position of lamps and furniture with plan-like precision. In a moment of mounting paranoia, I realised that the shiny blue metallic water bottle I was carrying might be mistaken for a hand-grenade.

'Listen, I'm really not doing anything dangerous here.' I pleaded.

They obviously weren't convinced and, after consulting amongst themselves for a minute or two, they marched me forwards towards the ashram gate.

'We're taking you to see the chief!'

Outside, the road was full of traffic and the pavements full of people: traders sat at their stalls while streams of fresh devotees continued to arrive at the ashram. But in my fear and confusion, I hardly noticed them. When we reached the police station I was told to sit down in the outer office.

'This is a Sai Baba police station!' announced one of the guards, pointing proudly to the enormous photo of the guru on the wall. I was not reassured. I had already heard one or two alarming stories of the fate awaiting those who fell foul of the great Sathya Sai spiritual organisation.

The policemen had some fun at my expense, ordering me to sketch a quick portrait of one of them before leading me upstairs to face the chief of police.

I stood in a dusty office, waiting anxiously in front of a paper-covered desk. A toilet flushed nearby. A few moments later, a huge man swaggered noisily into the room, snorting as he buttoned up his army-style trousers.

'Ah!' he boomed in a stern voice, looking me up and down, 'And what is your good name, Sir?'

I replied as calmly as I could.

'*Stein?*' He pronounced the word as if tasting something unpleasant. 'And tell me now, from which country do you hail?'

Good name? Hail? Was this guy for real? (I was yet to learn how many old-fashioned expressions survive in Indian English). But he was for real, and quizzed me thoroughly about my sketches, as well as inquiring into my reasons for visiting India and Puttaparthy. I wasn't sure how to answer. Was I a tourist? A traveller? An artist?

'We're going to have to check out your passport, Mr Stein.' There was a hint of menace in his voice.

'Will that take long?' I said, handing it over.

The chief shot me an imperious look. 'That's up to us! We do things properly here. You'll just have to wait.' He waved me out of the office as if I were a bothersome fly.

As one of the guards escorted me downstairs, I heard the

chief's voice shout behind me, 'And you can use your time here to think about what you are doing in our country!'

I was led to a small cell at the back of the police station.

'Is this really necessary?' I could feel the fear rising in my chest. Expressionless, the guard nudged me forwards and began to close the door. I turned to face the cell window through which a meagre slab of sunlight fell on a hard bench running along the wall. As the door slammed shut, I sat down and put my head in my hands. My first day in India and I was already in jail. How could things have gone wrong so quickly?

I recalled the flight from Heathrow and my first impressions of the country I had dreamed about for so long. As we touched down at Bangalore, the sun was rising hazily over distant hills. The air was warm and the light was soft. I stepped out of the plane, weary but excited, and set my feet on the sacred soil of India.

Mia, my contact at the ashram, had promised to send a driver to meet me. And there, on the other side of customs, amongst the crowd of Indians waiting for the new arrivals, was a smartly-dressed young man holding up a sign with the words 'Jon Spine' scrawled on it. He led me to an old-fashioned-looking cream car – the first of many Ambassadors I would ride in during my trip. After stowing my gear in the boot, we set off north into the countryside of Andhra Pradesh.

The sun had burned off the last of the morning mist and now cast a bright golden glow over the fields. Every detail, angle and colour seemed sharper. As we sped along, I felt I was moving in a Technicolor film-set. Huge, brightly painted lorries and rickety buses flew past us, hooting loudly. Cars, mopeds and bicycles weaved randomly between them, whilst dogs, goats and even a cow or two roamed freely across the road.

Dark-skinned men, women and children in bright, unfamiliar clothes seemed to be everywhere. Some drove animals or worked on half-built sections of the road along which we were travelling. Others stood outside shacks or sat on the pavement.

After an hour or so, we stopped at a roadside café and ate masala dosa – a large, thin rice pancake with a spicy potato filling. With us in the canteen was a crowd of lorry drivers. Sitting incongruously amongst them was a handful of middle-aged white women dressed in Indian clothes and wearing beatific expressions. They too were on their way to Prashanti Nilayam – the Abode of Peace.

As we approached Puttaparthy, the rocky terrain became greener. There were rice paddies being worked by ox-drawn ploughs, and some smartly dressed schoolchildren filing along the edge of the road. Coming into the town, we passed several grand buildings – hospitals, schools and museums – painted in cake-icing white, yellow and blue. Hanging outside them were huge posters of Sai Baba with his trademark orange robes and Afro hair-do. The large signs were subtitled with pithy maxims like "Patience is all the strength a man needs", and "Love all, serve all."

After being searched at the ashram gates, I was dropped off at the Overseas Visitor Accommodation Office where a gruff Indian official gave me instructions as to what I'd need during my stay. I was soon kitted out in a crisp, white shalwar kameez (cotton shirt and matching trousers), and had bought a meditation cushion and a thin mattress to sleep on. I also had my own little bit of floorspace in "Shed D22" – a bare, scruffy dormitory which was to be my home for the next week or so. I set up my pitch, fixed a mosquito net securely over the makeshift bed, and set out to explore.

It wasn't long until the next darshan with Sai Baba. I made my way to the mandir, the central temple, where a mass of people was already waiting for the guru. We sat quietly on the floor in rows and waited expectantly for Baba's appearance – some in meditation, others like me, restless, looking round at the faces, not quite sure what was going to happen. Minutes passed. Quarter of an hour, half an hour.

Still we waited.

As the tension continued to build, an electrifying charge suddenly went through the crowd. Swami (an affectionate title for the guru) had been spotted! But where was he? Was that him? At this distance I couldn't see much more than a small man dressed in orange, sitting in a wheelchair, surrounded by a group of attendants. Then, to the accompaniment of stirring music and impassioned chanting, the troupe began to make a circuit around the arena.

Happiness. That's the only word to describe the feeling that crashed, like an enormous wave, over us. The crowd began clapping and singing along. It was impossible not to be moved by the sheer joy that filled the temple. All around me, people were clambering to their feet. Some lurched forward, their arms outstretched, in an effort to petition their saviour; others tried simply to put themselves in the guru's line of sight. Meanwhile, a gaggle of hapless stewards ran back and forth waving their arms, shushing the noisier devotees, pushing others back into the crowd, and generally attempting to damp down the enthusiasm of the mob.

In the midst of it all sat Baba, looking absolutely oblivious to the commotion, a faint smile playing on his features. As he passed near me, I felt a powerful mixture of elation and fear. It was almost too strong to bear, and, after just a few moments more, I pressed my way out through the human mass into the fresh air beyond.

I walked until I felt calmer. And that was when I spotted the little temple dedicated to the elephant-headed god Ganesha. I'd seen a sign forbidding photography in the ashram, but assumed that sketching would be ok.

Now, I sat in jail – a prisoner of Sai Baba.

I heard the bolt slide on the door. The guard passed in a glass of water and a pamphlet. 'From the chief,' he said, then slammed the door again.

I opened the pamphlet. It was a little biography of the guru. I read that Baba was born in 1926 and had been a precocious child – excelling in singing, dancing and acting. After a serious illness and dramatic exorcism, the youth had recovered his health and declared himself to be an incarnation of the original Sai Baba – a Muslim fakir (holy man).

Having already performed minor miracles as a child – for example, producing sweets from nowhere for his friends – the young Baba began to draw crowds of followers attracted by tales of his wonder-working and wisdom. Later, he began to place more emphasis on teaching, and his healing mission expanded. The money from his followers helped fund new hospitals and schools, benefiting millions in rural India and elsewhere. Now, there were tens of millions of devotees spreading the good news all round the world.

It all seemed very impressive. But I knew too that Sai Baba and his organisation had come in for some criticism. Inevitably, there were stories of coercion, even violence, amidst the power struggles in this vast spiritual empire. More alarming still were the allegations of sexual abuse made by former devotees.

I closed the booklet and sat back. Had I really disobeyed the guru by sketching his shrine? I felt I'd done nothing wrong, but perhaps, after the recent bomb attacks in Mumbai, Indian security forces had a right to be twitchy. Still, I wondered if this wasn't just another example of the authoritarianism that seemed to characterise life around Sai Baba.

In the ashram, it seemed everything was governed by rules. Where you could walk, when you could eat, what you could buy… On top of that, the ashram staff often seemed indifferent and unfriendly. I didn't expect any special treatment, but on several occasions I'd felt snubbed by the very people purporting to be servants of a kind and loving guru. I'd been shushed in the library when I asked for the toilet, dismissed by an administrator after requesting a schedule of events, and

I'd got a filthy look from a chef in the canteen when I asked if there was a gluten-free option.

All this was far from the rose-tinted idea of ashrams I'd had in England. I'd seen pictures of the Beatles with the Maharishi; everyone blissed-out, wearing garlands, strumming guitars. They looked like they were having a great time. But I hadn't come to India as a hippy, or to drop out. I knew that I was, in my own way, sincere in my search. Yet I knew it wouldn't be easy to put aside my rational scepticism, or play by rules that seemed to me petty and pedantic.

Fifteen minutes later, the cell door swung open again. The chief stood above me, holding out my passport. 'It appears everything is in order, Mr. Stein. You have, I hope, had some time to think about your reason for visiting Puttaparthy?'

'Yes.' I replied, as humbly as I could.

'Jolly good. Well now, you are free to go.'

'And my sketchbook?'

'We shall hang on to that.'

'But –!'

'In case anything else comes to light,' he replied ominously. I let the matter drop and stepped out of the police station into the cool evening. The sudden sense of freedom was intoxicating. The hooting of the rickshaws, the smell of petrol and incense, the hand-painted shop signs, even the gaudy displays of religious tat in the tourist shops – I now appreciated it all in the light of liberty. As I turned back into the ashram, I smiled at the women squatting by the roadside with their displays of fruit, flowers and garlands. One smiled back at me and, in the warmth of the exchange, I resolved to give the ashram a second chance.

My enthusiasm didn't last very long. I got my first dose of "delhi-belly" and had to spend a couple of days making sure I didn't stray too far from a toilet. It also didn't help that Shed D22 was rapidly filling up with devotees arriving for Christmas.

At every hour of the day and night there was someone near me talking, whispering, or praying. I decided to leave the day after next.

Before going, I took the opportunity to do some seva (service) within the community – joining a friendly crew of international volunteers to help wash up. The atmosphere in the kitchen was convivial and the Brazilian man at the sink next to mine listened sympathetically as I told him what a rough time I'd had at the ashram.

'Each person gets the experience they need,' he said, passing me yet another thali dish to rinse.

I also made a solo trip into town where I visited a barber's shop and used an internet café. As I was returning to the ashram, an elderly and emaciated woman latched onto me, tugging at my sleeve as I walked along. She held on to my arm as her free hand moved to and from her mouth in a pitiful gesture of hunger. I tried to ignore her, but she would not be dismissed. Almost out of desperation, I took her into a grocer's shop and bought an enormous sack of rice, which she somehow manoeuvred onto her back.

I watched the ragged figure scuttle off, bent almost horizontal under the weight of the gift, and wondered if I had done the right thing. It was an extravagant gesture and the first of many uncomfortably mixed experiences of guilt and compassion prompted by the proximity of real poverty.

I hadn't yet managed to meet up with my contact, Mia, and so we arranged to meet in the town on my last morning. On my way out of the ashram I walked past rows of devotees waiting silently for darshan. I looked into the eyes of these simple Indian peasants and realized I would probably never understand their religious devotion. I was ashamed also to recognize a kind of scorn rising in me – mixed with pity – for what I perceived as their credulousness. I passed through the great gates and, despite the chaos of the street, felt relief to be out.

Meeting Mia at a café gave me an opportunity to share my recent experience with a devotee who had been involved with Sai Baba for many years. I decided not to mention getting arrested, but I did say that my visit to Prashanti Nilayam had not been altogether comfortable. I also confessed that I was probably too much of a sceptic to invest the guru with the significance others accorded him. Mia, in turn, related one or two anecdotes that to her, at least, confirmed Sai Baba's awesome status. We sipped our coffee in silence. As I got up to leave, I thanked her for helping me take my first steps in India.

'No problem, Jon. Have a safe trip. Sai Ram!'

Hesitantly, I returned the devotee's salute, then shouldered my rucksack and headed towards the bus-station. It was only eleven o'clock but I was already melting inside my clothes. The street was alive with noise and commotion but I felt calm inside. I was on the move again.

As I passed the police station, I dropped in a letter I'd written suggesting that sketching a temple probably represented a lesser threat to law and order than the potential hysteria of a huge crowd whipped up into religious frenzy. What the chief of police made of that idea I don't know, and I didn't hang around to find out – I had a bus to catch after all! For now, I was heading straight back to Bangalore, but where would I go then?

Bitten by the Cobra

As the bus rumbled out of Puttaparthy, I watched the evidence of Sai Baba's empire slip out of view. Within five minutes, the streams of devotees and monumental buildings had thinned out, leaving just a few giant posters of the smiling guru, advising us to "Go slow, take rest, travel safe."

Before leaving Britain, I'd heard horror-stories about riding buses in India but our vehicle seemed roadworthy, and the driver appeared to be in control of all his faculties. I relaxed back in to my seat.

The dusty road was lined with mud-thatched huts. Outside one of them, a woman stood bending over a bucket, washing her long black hair. Near her, half-naked children played with a mangy dog. Open fires burned in the streets while ox-drawn carts rumbled along, laden with cargo.

The bus trundled through a Muslim area that looked different from the surrounding Hindu villages. The settlement appeared neat and spacious, with its simple white and pastel-coloured buildings. Men in white skullcaps bustled around a mosque; elsewhere, groups of women in black headscarves seemed to glide along like ghosts.

As we approached Bangalore, I watched the open fields with their clusters of trees and huts give way to villages strung out along both sides of the road. Gradually, these straggly settlements mutated into a suburb of shops, offices and blocks of flats. The volume of people, traffic and noise was growing steadily. Garish advertising hoardings displayed urban India's new obsessions – cars, property, computers and jewellery. Soon we were traversing chaotic road junctions, flanked by tall buildings and neon signs. I had arrived in the city.

I decided to treat myself to a night of luxury and took a rickshaw from the bus station to a four-star hotel recommended in my guidebook. What a difference from the ashram! Here, the staff were friendly and attentive, everything was clean and I could even watch TV in my room.

After a good night's sleep and a hearty breakfast (including the ubiquitous idli – steamed rice rissole), I went out to explore the district round the hotel. Large modern shops sold kitchenware, clothes, books and mobile phones. Purposeful-looking Indians strode past me without even looking in my direction. After buying a sunhat and a replacement sketchbook, I returned to the hotel – already exhausted by the clamour and fumes of the street. I doubted if I would be any happier here than at Sai Baba's ashram and began to plan my onward journey.

I wanted to visit the historic city of Kochi (Cochin) in the south-western state of Kerala, but found out that there was a big festival happening there and little accommodation to be had. I decided instead to take the train to Mysore – a name that conjured exotic images of silk and sandalwood.

Even at midday, Bangalore railway station was heaving with people as if it were rush hour. Struggling under my rucksack, I managed to get a ticket and jostle my way to the packed platform. A ferocious jabber of shouts and cries rose up as the train pulled in and the crowd surged towards the carriage doors. In the mad rush for seats, I could even see children being handed in through the train windows. I dived into the general scrummage, let out a yell or two of my own, and finally got a seat.

As the train heaved out of the station, I got chatting to the smartly dressed Indian beside me. Chandru, an engineering student, was heading home to Mysore for the holidays. After asking me my name and my reasons for being in India, he shared his vision for his own life.

'When I finish my course, I will work in Bangalore,' he explained. 'Then I will marry. We will have a happy family and life will be good to us. This is the new India you know!'

Chandru exuded positivity and focus. He seemed supremely sure of himself and he was still only twenty-two! His dream was supported by a spiritual belief and discipline that I found impressive, but somewhat intense. From time to time I'd excuse myself from the conversation, make my way to the space between the carriages and lean out the window, feeling the wind and sunshine on my face. As the train trundled heavily along the tracks, I breathed in and out deeply, admiring the landscape of sun-baked farms, rolling to a horizon of low, blue hills. I waved to the workers in the wheat fields, some of whom beamed back at me in surprise, waving in turn.

When we arrived at Mysore, Chandru and I said goodbye.

'Good luck!' He waved as I sped off in a rickshaw. I was heading downtown to the Good Night hotel.

The place was a fleapit. My room was noisy and grubby, with wobbly furniture and a window that wouldn't open, but it would have to do for now. I unpacked a few things, fixed up my mosquito net and chained my rucksack to the bed. Tired as I was from the journey, I decided to head out straightaway.

The pavements were lined with cafés, chai shops and sweet-stalls, outside which stood crowds of men eating and drinking, chatting and smoking. As I walked, I breathed in a potent blend of cooking smells and exhaust fumes, with a whiff of animal dung and incense. I was soon lost among streets whose names I couldn't even find on the map I had torn from my guidebook.

'Sir, sir! You want help? I help you!' I looked round to see a wiry young Indian with a big grin on his face.

'No, I don't think so. I'm ok,' I said and strolled on. But he persisted, falling into step with me and keeping up his patter.

He extended his hand and introduced himself.

'I am Aslam. You come with me – I show you the city!'

I looked at him searchingly. He was not much beyond a teenager and, with his slightly scruffy clothes and dark good looks, he cut an attractive, if roguish figure. But could I trust him? I broached the subject of money but he dismissed my question with a smile, and a word that was to take on a humorous resonance between us.

'Shanti (peace), shanti, later you pay. Now we go!'

Within moments he had commandeered a rickshaw and we were speeding through the streets of old Mysore. Reassuring myself that the worst that could happen would be losing a few hundred rupees, I tried to relax into the adventure. After driving through a maze of side streets we stopped at a small house.

'This my friend. He a doctor – sell very good oil. You talk to him!'

I wasn't aware of having mentioned any health problems, but perhaps Aslam had picked up on an earlier comment of mine about looking for a yoga centre in the city. Either that, or he wanted to rack up some commission as quickly as possible. (I learned later of the arrangement between guides and local businesses in which the former get something for bringing visitors to the latter – whether there's a sale or not).

Stepping out of the heat into the cool interior of the house, I found myself in a gloomy consulting room. I sank into a huge, sagging sofa and looked around me at the piles of books, medical posters and bottles of oil.

An overweight middle-aged man appeared from behind a curtain and introduced himself as "Haman, the famous herbalist and palm-reader". He instructed a little child who had been poking his head round the doorway to go and get some chai.

Aslam slipped out on other business while Haman quizzed me as to the reason of my visit to India and my state of health.

I told him I was not looking for treatment, but he appeared so crestfallen that I decided, out of politeness more than anything else, to buy a few phials of oil. I chose some delightful smelling sandalwood, white jasmine and lotus. Then, without quite knowing how, I got talked into having my fortune read.

'Three women like you,' he told me as he studied the lines on my hands, 'and you are marrying twice!' His head wobbled with glee at the good news he was delivering. I wondered if I should tell him I was gay. Instead, I asked him whether he could see anything about the journey that lay ahead of me.

'Ah yes, the journey… ' He traced his finger along the lines of my palm. 'I see you are meeting with many obstacles on the way,' he said gravely. 'But, I think you are overcoming all such difficulties.' His finger had now reached the edge of my palm. 'When all is said and done, you are making a surprising victory.' A note of triumph appeared in his voice as he warmed to his subject, 'and your visit to India is a success!'

A surprising victory. A success. I couldn't quite imagine what he meant but it sounded promising. Just then, Aslam returned with more customers in tow. I shifted to make space for three tall Finnish men who could barely fit in the room. We were brought more tea and chatted briefly.

'How much do I owe you?' I asked Haman, getting up from my seat.

'Please you are paying Aslam later. Salaam aleikum.'

'Aleikum salaam,' I replied, and followed Aslam out into the sunlight.

'Very good, no? You like?' said Aslam, as he hailed another rickshaw for us.

'Well, it was … interesting,' I replied, 'but how much is all this costing me?'

Aslam beamed his mischievous grin at me, 'Shanti, shanti, Jon!'

I was not altogether comfortable with this system of running debts and insisted on sorting out payment for the morning's activities before accepting Aslam's suggestion to visit a few tourist sites. It wasn't a lot of money to spend, and I felt more secure having my own, personal guide.

It was early evening by the time we arrived back at the hotel. I was standing at reception waiting for my key, when, out of the corner of my eye, I saw something small and grey scurry past me up the staircase. 'Hey,' I cried, 'I've just seen a rat running up the stairs!'

'Don't worry,' replied the young man at the desk, without even looking up from his newspaper, 'he is living here.' Great! I thought, climbing the staircase on the lookout for other animals.

Back in my room, I checked to see if there was any way a rat could get in at night. I felt anxiety gnawing at me. Would I be attacked? Just how hungry were the rodents here? I hadn't come to India for luxury, but I drew the line at sharing my room with vermin. I reassured myself that tomorrow I would be out of here. I blocked up the gap under the door with some clothes and tried to get some sleep.

Next morning I was up and out early to meet Aslam. We took a rickshaw out from the city centre to the luxurious suburb of Laxshmipuram whose wide, leafy streets were flanked with smart, colonial-era houses. Tucked down a quiet side street, in a large old bungalow, was the Mandala Yogashara (yoga centre) which would be my home for the next few weeks.

I said goodbye to Aslam and passed through to a tiny office where Shantala, the administrator, signed me up for a weeklong course of yoga and pranayama (breathing exercises). She took me round to the café at the back of the centre where a crowd of fit-looking students from around the world were unwinding in between classes.

Next, she led me to an accommodation block comprising individual units, each with its own bathroom and tiny kitchen. I took in the low wooden cot, chipped enamel sink and one-ring gas burner and felt I could be happy living here.

'Surya namaskara!'

I groaned inwardly. I hate the sun-salute – especially at seven o'clock in the morning. Half-heartedly, I thrust my right leg back into a lunge. But Ramesh, my yoga teacher, was taking no nonsense.

'I think you are being able to do better than that, Mr Jon!'

Ramesh was a short, barrel-chested Indian whose shy smile and soft voice belied his iron discipline in the yoga hall. There were just two other students in the class. On one side of me was a German girl, Claudia, leaping athletically into contortions I had never imagined possible. On the other, Noam, a longhaired Israeli, who moved even slower than I did. I struggled on my mat, trying to focus on the demanding drill of asanas (yoga poses) I was being shown.

After a few days of classes I began to feel more confident. In fact, I started to get a little carried away with myself. One morning, as I stretched nonchalantly into the cobra pose, I felt a sudden sharp tearing in my chest. I cried out and fell back to the ground, my limbs splayed awkwardly.

'That is not correct posture, Mr Jon.' Ramesh stood over me, tutting as I lay groaning on the floor.

'But –!' I gasped.

'No excuses! The cobra is always biting those who are not showing sufficient respect for it.'

I was placed under the care of a young doctor trained in ayurveda (Indian natural medicine), who advised me to stop classes and gave me a treatment regime which consisted of massaging an aromatic oil onto my chest and taking some herbal remedy. This helped a little, but the pain in my chest persisted.

Despite my injury, I was enjoying life at the Mandala and Mysore. Most days, I got up early and went out walking as the sun was beginning to rise over the city. The temples were already welcoming devotees making the morning puja – the traditional offerings to the gods of fruit and flowers. Brightly-dressed women were out, sweeping in front of their houses or rinsing clothes, and smartly dressed children were on their way to school – smiling or laughing as they walked. The streets were beginning to fill with cars, rickshaws, buses and bikes flowing in every direction. The chai-sellers and snack-stalls that lined the pavements were already doing brisk business. And, amongst all this human activity, ambled cows and an occasional calf, munching at the piles of refuse in the streets. I also spotted horses, dogs, cats, goats, squirrels and even monkeys. Surprisingly few rats though – perhaps they prefer hotel life…

I was also hanging out with some of the other students. Amongst the guys in particular, there was a curious mixture of serious yoga practice and even more serious dope-smoking going on. When I took a puff on a joint I usually found the experience slightly alarming. Did that hill on the horizon really look so big and bright yesterday? Did I even see it?

On one occasion, after smoking together, I accompanied two Israeli friends into a poor Muslim area nearby. Within seconds, a gang of children had descended upon us, joking and laughing and clamouring to see themselves photographed with a digital camera. But I felt uncomfortable, guilty even – a (relatively) rich, stoned tourist strolling through a humble Indian neighbourhood.

My sense of paranoia was fed by some nearby posters with Arabic-looking writing. Then I saw what appeared to be a blood-red star of David, daubed on the wall of a house. Chilled by the sight, I experienced a flashback to a time in Jerusalem, many years ago, when I got lost in an Arab area outside the city walls. A mob of Palestinians had surrounded me and I began to fear for my life, until one enterprising youngster offered to lead me to safety – for a fee, of course.

Here I was, once again, lost and trapped in a hostile

neighbourhood. I had to get out! Then the laughter of children brought me back to my senses. I looked at my Israeli friends and once again we were just three stoned tourists. The fear soon passed (with the assistance of some chai), but that was it for dope-smoking in India. Any more highs would have to come naturally.

Christmas came and went with very little fuss. New Year followed with fireworks and a small celebration with the other students. I had tentatively started yoga classes again, but my injury had not fully healed. I was not sure whether to stay in Mysore or go on with my journey. Since I was not on a schedule, I could see the potential to drift – living cheaply in a privileged bubble while allowing a sense of timelessness to dull the sharper aspects of life. I recalled my original intention to stop in Mysore only until I could find somewhere to stay in Kochi. Over three weeks later I still hadn't left!

But Kerala was a long way away and I could afford to take a few days to get there. I asked other travellers what places they recommended seeing and decided to head to the tea-plantations and hill stations of the Nilgiris (Blue Mountains) a few hours south. I lined up accommodation in Ootacamund, or Ooty, as the place has come to be known, and began to get excited about moving on.

On my last evening, I had a little farewell party with my yoga buddies. It was a warm moonlit night. Sandalwood incense wafted through the candle-lit café in the centre's garden as a small crowd of us gathered to chat, eat and share songs. Ramesh joined us too. With representatives from England, France, Israel, Russia, Australia, Germany and India we created our own little mandala under the stars.

The next morning, I packed my stuff and cleared my room. There was just one more person to say goodbye to. Over the few weeks I stayed at the Mandala I'd kept in touch with Aslam who had arranged several outings for me. He came to see me off at the bus station. Pride and joy lit up his face. 'Tomorrow I am to be marrying,' he announced. 'Soon I will have a wife and a shop!'

I was happy for him, but amazed too – he seemed so young. I made him a wedding present of my old mobile phone and he, seeking to return the gesture, went off and bought me a spicy samosa with chilli sauce. (Unfortunately I forgot to take the SIM card out of the phone and still, to this day, people occasionally tell me they've tried to contact me on my old number, only to be greeted by a puzzled Indian, offering to sell them anything from hair-oil to incense).

It was time to board the bus. But which one? Coaches and buses, people and luggage were mixed up in a noisy circus of engines and shouting. Everyone, from the newborn to the most decrepit, was getting ready for a journey. Officials strolled around imperiously, barking instructions to no one in particular.

Aslam went off to find out where I should go as I surveyed the chaos around me. Five minutes later he reappeared and pointed to a particularly rusty, battered-looking coach. Paint was peeling from the bonnet and several windows were missing. Someone was clambering on the roof, tying luggage haphazardly to a rack. Clusters of passengers, clutching bags and babies, were boarding. I followed them, having decided to keep my rucksack with me, and took a seat at the front.

Half an hour later the driver put in an appearance. He was a short, paunchy man, fiftyish, and appeared to have come straight from a long night out on the town. Unshaven, bleary-eyed and sweaty, he plumped down into his seat, made a perfunctory inspection of the mirrors and regarded the controls in front of him as if he had never operated a vehicle before. At last, he cajoled the old coach into life and, as we sputtered out of the bus station, I waved goodbye to Aslam and Mysore.

I sat back and watched with some relief as the city slowly fell away and the Indian countryside welcomed me once again. What, I wondered, would the Blue Mountains hold for me? First though, I would have to survive the bus journey – which would prove an adventure in itself.

3

The Queen of Hill Stations

The bus weaved south through the Bandipur National Park. Road signs warned of wild animals, including man-eating tigers, but the only wildlife I saw was one very tame-looking baby elephant. In any case, my attention was fixed on the driver who divided his time between yawning and stretching in his seat, sounding his horn, and adjusting the radio beside him to keep his favourite music station tuned in.

No one else appeared to share my anxiety about the state of the driver, or the condition of the bus. In fact, despite us jolting along a potholed road to the usual accompaniment of blaring horns and shrieking brakes, many of the other passengers were already dozing contentedly. But there would be no sleep for me.

I watched helplessly through the front windscreen as other buses and lorries thundered towards us. The drivers seemed to be playing a deadly game of "chicken", with the larger vehicles toughing it out for dominance on the road, holding their course and forcing the approaching traffic to swerve and give way. Often the gap between passing vehicles was no more than a hand's breadth, and the roadside was littered with the wrecks of vehicles that had veered off into the ditch. After a half-hour of this white-knuckle ride I could bear it no longer.

'Do you think you could slow down a little please?' I shouted across the gangway.

The driver swivelled his head to face me. 'Good sir, you are in India,' he called back, his face bearing a diabolic grin, 'and it is we who are in charge now!'

A shiver of terror ran through me. We had a long journey ahead and I wondered if we would make it intact.

The hill-station town of Ooty is over 2,500 feet up in an area rich with tea plantations. As the road began to climb and bend, the landscape transformed into a scene of pines, streams and meadows – not unlike Scotland. But the view from the side-window of the bus was now as alarming as that from the front. Just inches from the side of the potholed tarmac the land disappeared in a scrotum-shrivelling drop down the mountainside. The sporadic barriers, all rusted and broken, did no more than indicate where some other unfortunates had already flown over the cliff face into oblivion.

I glanced anxiously towards the man at the wheel. His head was nodding periodically and I assumed he was just keeping time with the Bollywood hits blaring from the radio. But now I watched with mounting horror as every couple of minutes he would come to with a jolt and throw the steering wheel one way or the other, scarcely looking ahead at the traffic. The bastard was dozing off!

'Hey!' I shouted, each time I saw the driver's head begin to dip. But he hardly seemed to register my cries. Meanwhile, the passengers behind me continued acting in blissful ignorance of the danger we were in. Most were fast asleep: those that remained awake bumped along reading their newspapers or eating. My nerves were already shredded by the time we stopped for a break at a roadside café. As I carried my chai away from the counter, I noticed the driver standing nearby tucking into a samosa.

'Listen,' I said, as politely as I could, 'I couldn't help noticing that you seem very tired. Is it really wise to drive in that condition?'

He drew himself up to his full five feet and fixed me with

a withering look. 'I am driving twenty-five years with the Tamil Nadu Corporation of Public Transport. Twenty-five years I tell you! And in all that time I have been involved in only fifteen motor accidents.' He paused as if waiting for me to congratulate him on the statistic.

'Er, that's very… impressive,' I said, fearing becoming involved in the sixteenth. Then, a flash of inspiration. 'Look, can I buy you a coffee?'

His face softened. 'Most certainly. Gifts of tea and coffee from customers always acceptable under company regulations. Cigarettes and alcohol prohibited!'

I went back to the counter and asked the chai-wallah to make me the strongest cup of coffee possible. I then added several teaspoons of sugar and prayed that the treacly mixture would keep the driver awake for the rest of the journey.

By now it was early evening. The sun had fallen low, leaving us hurtling along in a dim twilight. Through the bus windows came the cool smell of damp pine. Ahead of us, the mountain route meandered in near-darkness, illuminated only by headlights. Were we even on the right side of the road anymore? The bus interior was dark, but a dim bulb continued to flicker over the driver; in the half-light, his lolling form cast unearthly shadows around the cab. Pounding drums and shrieking voices continued to spew from the radio. There was nothing for me to do but give up, let go, and trust in the Gods.

We can't have been too far from our destination when I heard the long scream of a horn, and saw a flashing of lights through the windscreen. Then a crashing jolt and the scraping crumple of metal on metal. Our bus juddered and swerved, throwing us sideways in our seats. The driver was trying frantically to steady the vehicle. *This is it,* I thought, preparing to say my prayers. I envisaged a last, dramatic flight over the cliff-edge. But no. There came instead the rumbling of wheels on earth, the scratch of vegetation along the windows, and another crashing sound with which the vehicle came to a stop.

The sudden stillness was ruptured by the hiss of an engine leaking steam. I noticed that the radio had, mercifully, been silenced. Then came a great eruption of noise from the rudely awakened passengers behind me: babies crying, women wailing and men shouting. The driver was slumped over his wheel, but he was not to enjoy more than a moment's rest as several young men came yelling down the aisle, pushed and prodded him, and finally manhandled him out of his seat and off the bus. Other passengers followed, their voices combining in a chorus that filled the night.

I stepped down from the bus and felt the cool, fragrant humidity of the air. We had come off the road into a stand of eucalyptus trees. Gaslights from small houses glowed nearby and knots of people were already gathering around the bus. Luggage had tumbled off the roof and passengers were turning over boxes and sorting through bags. A fight had broken out around the driver who was feebly trying to shield himself from the punches of a youth. Others looked on, shouting, while just behind the circle of combatants a couple of old women were sitting down on boxes, calmly unwrapping food for the children who stood around them. The atmosphere was somewhere between a wrestling match and a picnic. I felt tired and hungry, and relieved to be still alive.

After a few minutes a policeman arrived and attempted to restore law and order. The bruised driver was taken away to the village, muttering unintelligibly amidst a hail of spitting and curses.

'So what happens now?' I asked a young man standing next to me.

'Coming soon is other bus. We are waiting here.'

It was past eleven o'clock when we finally arrived at Ootacamund bus station. Exhausted and nervy, I got a taxi to take me to the YWCA. I barely registered my surroundings as I checked in and found my room. I got straight into bed and passed an uneasy night, filled with dreams of speeding and swerving, and fractured images of luggage tumbling over me.

The following morning I looked through my window on a scene more alpine than Indian. The YWCA was perched high on a hillside and comprised a series of chalets positioned around an old, whitewashed chapel. There were trees, grass and flowers, and neatly-clipped hedges marking off tidy lawns. At the foot of the hill lay an old racecourse, scrubby and unused. On the slopes around the town were small fields that had been converted into market gardens. Pine trees filled the skyline, silhouetted against the distant mountains. The sky was a radiant blue.

The atmosphere inside the hostel was how I imagine a girls' boarding school might have felt like in the 1950s. Everything was neat and clean, the decor and furniture simple. Upstairs was a reading-room whose bookcases were filled with romantic novels in English and French; next-door, a draughty lounge with an old upright piano in the corner. There were prints of impressionist masterpieces, and framed watercolours of healthy-looking young women (all Western) in summer dresses and straw hats. It seemed to be house policy to leave all the doors and windows open, and by nightfall the place was like a fridge.

I spent a couple of days mooching round the town, visiting the beautiful botanical gardens and government rose-garden (which boasts 20,000 varieties), and doing the usual rounds of shops, markets and temples. One compensation for the lower temperature in Ooty was the abundance of chocolate – sold all over the place and in such a variety of flavours that it was hard to choose which to buy first. I have a vivid, if slightly surreal, memory of spending an afternoon at the "Regal Picture House" watching *The Day the Earth Stood Still* (original language with Hindi subtitles) – calmly gorging on mint chocolate while the planet was decimated by tiny metallic monsters.

Another comfort was tea, which, though no longer cultivated in Ooty itself, is still grown at lower altitudes throughout the region. I took a tour around a former tea-factory; watching how the stuff is manufactured, and learning something of the role this simple crop has played in world trade and politics. For example, the East India Tea Company, founded in 1698, represents the beginning of Britain's imperial designs, and the Boston Tea Party was a catalyst for the American War of Independence. (On a more trivial note, I learned that our word 'tips' stands for 'to inspire prompt service').

The Regal cinema, cups of tea, botanic gardens and chocolate – there were echoes of the British Raj everywhere. One evening I had just taken my seat in the chilly dining-room when I heard the clangourous sound of scales being practised on the piano upstairs. They sounded suspiciously like the majors and minors that form part of the standard training in Western classical music. Curiosity took me up to the lounge, where an Indian boy sat at the yellowing keyboard. I waited at the doorway for a moment, then went in.

'Oh, I hope I am not disturbing you sir,' he said.

'Not at all. I like to listen.'

Thomas told me he was fifteen and was studying for his Grade 3 Associated Board grade exam.

'Are you playing any Bach?' I asked him.

'Who?'

'Bach… J. S. Bach! You've got to know some Bach if you play the piano. Here, listen to this.'

Coincidentally, I had taken a piano exam myself not long before leaving the UK, and so was able to give a passable performance of a prelude and fugue. I let the last triumphant chord fade away and turned back to the young pianist. 'Well, did you like it?'

He frowned, then paused for a moment as if choosing his words carefully. 'Sir, it was very good and all, but tell me, can you perform the D major scale over two octaves?'

Back at the dinner table, I mused on my failure to communicate the marvels of baroque polyphony to an Indian. But perhaps such harmonically complex music is strange for someone who has grown up within a completely different musical culture. Maybe there is a tendency in the West to think of our artistic achievements as representing humanity as a whole – it was music by Bach, after all, that was sent out into space with the Apollo mission. But now the Indians have their own space programme, perhaps the sound of tablas and sitars too is echoing across the Universe.

Despite firmly shutting my bedroom window and using my sleeping bag, I couldn't sleep for the cold, and woke each morning with the pain in my rib playing its old song. I wanted to be warm again and decided to move on as quickly as possible to coastal Kerala.

I managed to get a ticket that afternoon for the so-called "Toy Train" – the narrow gauge steam railway that threads a winding route down the mountains from Ooty. After a tortuous descent lasting several hours, we reached the town of Mettupalayam. I stepped out of the threadbare compartment into the humid evening, sooty and grimed from the smoke that had blown into the carriage as we went.

Travelling on another train from there, I stayed a night in the industrial city of Coimbatore. In the hotel room I unpacked my toiletries and found the little brown bottle of oil I'd bought at a dispensary in Ooty. The assistant there had been very persuasive, and in a moment of uncharacteristic anxiety over my baldness, I'd succumbed to vanity.

'Complete hair restoration in just six applications!' she'd promised.

Unfortunately, she didn't tell me that the oil needed to be diluted. (The instructions on the bottle were written in an indecipherable Indian script). Oh well, I thought, stepping into the shower, the more the better! I splashed a handful of the oil on my head and about three seconds later a burning sensation started across my scalp. Over the next couple of minutes, the heat around my skull built to such a crescendo that I was practically hopping around the bathroom in a state of panic. I kept dousing my head with cold water but nothing seemed to help. Should I call reception and ask for a doctor? Shanti, shanti, I told myself. More splashing myself with cold water. I even drank a couple of glasses hoping to cool myself from the inside out.

After ten or fifteen minutes the worst of it had passed. I looked in the mirror and apart from some redness, there seemed to be no permanent damage. Eventually my scalp calmed down and I went to bed imagining my head gently glowing in the dark. Looking in the bathroom mirror the next day, I observed no new growth, but was relieved to find what hair I did possess still attached to my head. It did look a slightly odd ginger colour though.

To reach Kerala from Coimbatore, I would have to take a bus. At the bus station I went through the usual rigmarole of trying to find the right booth to buy my ticket, queueing for ages, then waiting even longer for the delayed bus. Thankfully, both vehicle and driver looked roadworthy. I decided this time to sit near the back, as I couldn't bear to witness any more near collisions. As we pulled away from the noisy terminal, I settled into my seat, and read up a little about Cochin and Kerala.

I was looking forward to being by the sea, amongst tourists, soaking up the history and culture of this ancient port. I wondered, too, if I might now find some guidance and healing on my journey of discovery. Didn't the famous "hugging guru", Amma, live down here somewhere? I was a month into my trip and in sore need of some human warmth and inspiration. And I was, indeed, to find a little of each – though not quite in the way I'd imagined.

4

Relaxing at Fort Kochi

In comparison with the nightmare journey to Ooty, the bus ride to Kerala was positively benign. There was still plenty of hooting and swerving in the road, but it was, at least, daylight and we were travelling on the flat. The bus sped past field after field of tall palms, lending the scene a jungle-like appearance. As we approached the coast, the humidity increased until I was sweating in my seat.

We reached the modern city of Ernakulum which stands opposite the historic port of Kochi (formerly Cochin), across an estuary of the Arabian Sea. From the bus station I had a long rickshaw ride to Fort Kochi – the centre of the former European enclave founded by the Portuguese in 1500. The driver left me in an area of leafy streets and old buildings with grand, faded façades and antique window-shutters.

I had booked a "homestay" (B+B style accommodation, often within the proprietor's own house) in advance, and now found my way to George and Maria's around the corner from the town's main junction. George had the slow, soft-spoken gentleness of many of the Keralans I was to meet, and showed me a clean, simple room on the first floor. The rent was not cheap, but I liked the place and paid for a week in advance.

Fort Kochi had a relaxed, friendly flavour. People rode around on bicycles, the streets and pavements were clean, and there were tourist shops, trendy cafés and bijou hotels galore. It may not have been the "real" India, but at least I felt safe here. I looked at the sea, the port, and the fishermen plying their enormous traditional Chinese nets, and couldn't wait to start sketching.

Each morning I went out into the cool, quiet streets to buy fruit and other supplies. Then, after meditating back in my room, I would take my breakfast up to the roof terrace where great black crows eyed me hungrily. Keralans are not allowed to build above three or four storeys, and so from my vantage point I could look out over the district and watch life unfolding as people started their day. Opposite my homestay was a building site where men and women were heaving stones about, hammering metal or drilling into bare rock. Not a single one of them wore a helmet – and most went barefoot.

I hired a bike and spent hours cycling around the district, stopping to sightsee, sketch or mooch in the shops and cafés. It was a little easier here to meet fellow travellers; I hung out with Natan from Israel, fresh from the army, and later ran into Eric – a charming gay New Yorker whom I'd already met in Mysore. But I still had plenty of time on my hands and it wasn't long before I started feeling restless and lacking in purpose.

For some reason, the thought of searching out another guru or ashram had lost its appeal. I had heard about the remains of an ancient Jewish community at Cochin and wondered if revisiting my own religious roots might hold a clue in my spiritual search.

My guidebook informed me that Jews are reputed to have landed on the Keralan coast after the destruction of the temple in Jerusalem in 70 CE. They enjoyed good relations with the local Indian rulers and prospered, and in 1568 they built their synagogue at the trading post of Matancherry – not far from Fort Kochi.

That afternoon, I cycled towards the part of Matancherry still known as "Jew Town". The streets were lined with shops bursting with great sacks of food; mostly rice, beans and spices. Traders came and went, dealing with one another at desks set up in the open shop-fronts.

At the end of a quiet, shady lane lay the synagogue. There was little to be seen from the outside, but as I passed through the main doors I felt myself stepping back in time. The spacious, airy hall was charged with an atmosphere of antiquity and stillness. In the centre stood the bimah – the railed platform from where the Law is read each Sabbath; and there, on the far wall, was the Ark containing the Torah scrolls. Around the edges of the hall ran the rows of benches for the male worshippers, while overlooking us, from behind, was the screened-off women's gallery on the first floor. A multitude of glass oil-lamps hung down from the ceiling, lending an exotic touch to the sober interior.

My mood of contemplative appreciation was soon shattered by a wave of tourists rushing in with a great whoosh of excitement, aiming their cameras at one or two artefacts, then flowing back out again.

I returned the following evening, a Friday, hoping to attend the Sabbath service.

'Are you Jewish?' asked a stooped, elderly man at the doorway.

'Yes, I am.' I looked straight into his suspicious eyes.

'What is your name? Where do you come from? Where do you pray?'

I hadn't expected an interview and answered him curtly. I was also irritated to see one or two other men (wearing skullcaps, admittedly) being admitted without question. Yet wasn't the man justified in checking my credentials? Should I have assumed that being born Jewish gave me an automatic right to entrance?

As it was, there were barely enough of us to conduct a proper service. I don't know what I'd hoped for, but by the end I felt disappointed. The mumbled and hurried prayers in Hebrew, the chants intoned in a haphazard dirge, and the overall sense of hacking through a thicket of overgrown liturgy — it was all too familiar from the Orthodox Judaism I'd grown up with.

I reminded myself I was probably witnessing the last gasps of a dying community – most of the last members of the former Jewish colony of Cochin emigrated to Israel years ago. But what a tantalizing thought to imagine a service a century or two back – the building packed with smartly-dressed worshippers, a cantor intoning the holy texts to an oriental melody, and who knows, perhaps even an inspiring sermon!

Unbelievably, the pain in my rib had still not gone away. If anything, it seemed to be getting worse, and sometimes, waking in the morning, I found I could hardly move my body without excruciating pains shooting through my abdomen.

I decided to seek medical attention and turned up early the next day at the government hospital in Fort Kochi. Several basic buildings (some even lacking windows) stood around a sandy courtyard. A few elderly women were sweeping in doorways. I was among the first patients to arrive and took my place on a wooden bench in a bare waiting room. An administrator sold me a two-rupee ticket admitting me to the surgery next-door – a spartan, high-ceilinged hall divided up amongst three doctors who sat behind battered desks whilst patients presented themselves. Everything happened in the open; there was no privacy.

I stripped off my shirt for the doctor to inspect my chest. He looked, prodded, and listened to it with a stethoscope, then wrote out an order for an x-ray to be taken. 'Have I broken something?' I asked in alarm.

'I don't think so,' replied the doctor, 'but it's best to be sure.' He handed me a slip of paper and directed me to the radiology department. I crossed the courtyard and entered a dim shed that was empty except for a bench and an antiquated x-ray machine. As I sat down and waited for the radiologist to arrive I heard what sounded like hymns being sung outside. Through the doorway I could see an assembly of hospital staff, gathered to worship together before work. I wondered at this religious display within the health service – faith and medicine obviously still worked hand in hand here.

A few minutes later, the radiologist came and prepared me for the x-ray. At the push of a button, the old machine whirred and clanked into life. Then it stopped again. Mutterings from the radiologist and more button-pushing. Was this thing safe, I asked myself, and if not, was I being exposed to massive amounts of radiation?

An hour later, when I picked up the developed images, the radiologist said there was no evidence of any broken bones, but that there was a shadowy area that might indicate infection. Anxiously, I took the negative back to the doctor who told me it was nothing serious and not to worry. He prescribed me a course of analgesics but I was still not satisfied. Back at my homestay, I asked George for some advice. He suggested going to the bigger and better-equipped Hospital Trust in Ernakulum.

The next day I took the ferry across to the city. What a contrast to quaint, pretty Fort Kochi! The afternoon was sweltering and I nearly exhausted myself traversing traffic-filled streets and packed pavements. At last, I found the hospital – a large, modern facility catering for tourists and foreign visitors as well as the better off in the local population.

Inside, there was a barrage of bureaucracy to negotiate, but I eventually got to see a young doctor who asked to look at the x-ray I'd brought from the Government Hospital.

'It's that shadowy bit I'm worried about,' I said, handing the negative to him. He held it up to the light.

'Mr Stein,' he chuckled, 'there is absolutely no need for you to be feeling any alarm. That shadow is your heart!'

He suggested that I'd probably torn a muscle and then he prescribed a cocktail of drugs to soothe and mask the pain. I left the hospital relieved at being spared the diagnosis of a terminal illness, but concerned as to why my injury was not healing as fast as I would have liked. It had not yet dawned on me that my anxiety about my condition was being fed by culture-shock, as well as the loneliness and strain of having to organize and process every aspect of my daily experience in this overwhelmingly foreign country.

I never seriously doubted my decision to come to India or thought of flying home, but now, after six weeks away, I did start to question what I was actually here for. Was I on a spiritual quest, or just taking an exotic holiday? Either way, why wasn't I enjoying myself a bit more?

The next morning, in a café in Fort Kochi, I got an answer – of sorts. On a shelf near my table was a familiar-looking book about meditation. As I flicked through it, I recalled my very first steps on the spiritual path. Like many teenagers, I'd been intrigued by supernatural and psychic phenomena. It was a time when Uri Geller was still performing on television and the film *Close Encounters* had reawakened interest in UFOs. With friends, I had attempted a séance and, at home, had dabbled with a deck of Tarot cards.

There was a more serious side to my searching too. Through my Jewish upbringing I had become aware of a mystical tradition, that is, the esoteric or hidden side of religion which emphasizes the personal, inner experience of the Divine more than communal worship and outward ritual. A sympathetic cousin gave me a copy of Kahlil Gibran's "The Prophet" which presented a view of life at once poetic and paradoxical. I began to feel there must be more to life than what I was seeing around me, and what I was being told by my parents and teachers.

I went to a public lecture on Transcendental Meditation (TM) and, over the following weeks, practised using a mantra to calm the mind. There were no mystical revelations, but one morning, on the way to school, I was struck by the sudden and uncommon beauty of the trees against the autumn sky. Everything had a clarity and vividness I'd not noticed before.

Whatever angst my adolescence might have been bringing me, the world seemed essentially good. Though the experience soon faded, the memory of that brief, direct perception remained clear.

My encounter with TM also gave me my first taste of the uneasy relationship between spirituality and commerce. At the end of the introductory course the group was invited to participate in an advanced training. I was shocked at how expensive it was. 'I'm sorry, but I'm still at school,' I said. 'There's no way I can afford that!'

'Don't worry,' came the reply, 'it's only the icing on the cake.'

That's pretty expensive caster sugar, I thought, but my cynicism did not prevent me from pursuing my interest in spiritual matters. I bought joss sticks and a second-hand copy of the Bhagavad Gita (which I did not get very far with), and read my first book on meditation and the spiritual life – trying to put into practice some of the ideas suggested by the Keralan author.

Now, twenty-five years later, here I was, sitting in a café looking at a copy of the same book.

I took the coincidence as an auspicious sign. Have a little faith, I told myself. I sensed vaguely that there might be a bigger pattern behind the events of my journey: I just couldn't see it yet. Despite my pain, fatigue and anxiety, it was not yet time to give up. Hadn't Hamid the fortune-teller told me I'd encounter many obstacles on the way, yet find success in the end? Happily, there was some help just around the corner

The Science of Life

It was a hot, late afternoon and I was on my way back from Vypeen Island — a beach area not far from Kochi. My attention was drawn to the shopfront of a small clinic. "Dr Mini – Ayurvedic Treatment" read the sign.

Ayurveda (literally "science of life") is a five-thousand-year-old system of traditional medicine practised widely in India and elsewhere. I'd already noticed lots of little dispensaries and clinics on my travels, but now something prompted me to cross the road and see what actually went on inside.

I entered a small consulting room surrounded by shelves filled with bottles, jars and herbal products. A plumply attractive woman behind a desk smiled at me and invited me to sit down. 'Good afternoon, I am Doctor Mini,' her voice was low and rolled like honey from her full lips, 'how can I help you?'

I introduced myself and told her about the pain in my chest. She asked some questions about my general health and suggested a treatment known as panchakarma – massage with herbal oils, accompanied by steam baths. She said the combination would not only deal with the immediate muscle pain, but could also help with chronic fatigue. In my case, she said, the process would also involve hot rice and milk.

I was intrigued. Dr Mini was warm and friendly, and though she was a little vague about the cost of the treatment, seemed trustworthy. I pictured myself spread out on a couch, relaxing under Mini's capable fingers, and later nibbling on warm rice pudding. I asked her when I could start and she invited me to accompany her there and then to the clinic at her home in Pallaruthy, a suburb of Kochi. We negotiated a price and set off in a rickshaw.

It seemed a very long journey, and we stopped twice en route: once at a Catholic shrine for Mini to make an offering, and then again in a busy suburb for her to buy someone a birthday present. Sitting waiting in the rickshaw, I had plenty of time to wonder if I was being led on a wild goose chase. But I was learning to go with the flow in such situations and sat back, taking in the sights and sounds of the streets.

Soon, we entered a leafy suburban district and stopped at a bungalow set back from the road. Mini invited me inside and indicated a chair in an anteroom decorated with family photographs. I could hear the sound of a television coming from the next room and, after a few moments, two young children – a boy and a girl – poked their heads shyly around the doorway. Mini returned and I stood up, ready to follow her to wherever the treatments were given.

'Sit down, Jon. Relax. Joppen will be here shortly.'

'Joppen?'

'Yes, he is giving you the treatment. In ayurveda only men are allowed to massage men.'

Just as I was adjusting my mental image from Mini to that of a lithe young masseur (preferably oiled himself), clad in a loincloth and gliding his hands over me, a short dark bear of a man shambled in. He was at least sixty and, with his soiled white singlet, unshaven face and a beedi (cheap, strong Indian cigarette) hanging from his mouth, he did not inspire much confidence as a healthcare practitioner. He smiled broadly and extended his hand.

'I'm afraid Joppen is unable to speak or understand any English,' said Mini. With a weak smile, I offered my hand back, which he took in a crushing handshake. Dear God, I thought,

What have I let myself in for?

I waited a little longer while Joppen went to prepare oils for the massage, then went round the house to join him in the "treatment room" – a battered, wooden outhouse in the garden. Inside, it was dark and smelled of kerosene. A gaudy statue of Jesus smiled down from a shelf, candles around its feet. In the middle of the room stood an enormous massage table, high off the ground and made from solid wood.

Joppen attempted to communicate with me through a system of grunts and gestures. I got undressed and put on the flimsiest of loincloths (basically two strips of fabric ripped off an old sheet – one going round and one going under). Climbing onto the table was agony. I gasped and groaned as I hoisted myself up into a lying position. Things eased slightly as the massage began – Joppen working long, strong strokes up and down my whole body, from the foot right up to the shoulder. As he mumbled to himself, I began to relax and enjoy the experience. Besides, there was rice pudding to look forward to afterwards.

The door opened briefly and someone handed in a parcel. I caught a strong, but appetizing odour of cooked milk, rice and herbs. I looked up to see Joppen advancing towards me with a plump, steaming bag. Would I eat so soon? And in here? Alas, no. He signalled for me to turn onto my front and, in the next moment, I felt him pummelling my back with the bag.

I endured ten disappointing minutes of this fragrant pounding before climbing off the table and stepping into a large wooden cabin. This was the steam bath, operated by a burner on the floor that heated water and piped the vapour into the box. Joppen secured the door, replaced the lid with my head sticking through the head hole, muttered something, and went out.

Five minutes passed. Ten minutes. I sat in the contraption, in the darkness, getting hotter and hotter. Jesus was shimmering eerily in the flickering candlelight. I was almost passing out from the heat and ready to shout for help when the door opened. Joppen came in and switched off the burner. Then he led me to a cubicle at the back of the outhouse where I soaped myself and washed off with a hot bucket shower. When I emerged into the garden, dusk had fallen and all was peaceful. I felt I'd just run a marathon. But along with the exhaustion came a strange sense of cleansing and refreshment.

Unlike the weekly or monthly massage that we might take in the West, ayurveda treatments tend to be given daily over a shorter, intensive period. I wanted to stick with the treatment, but Mini's suggestion of coming each day for a fortnight meant a lot of travelling (it was at least an hour's journey either way from my homestay). It wasn't cheap either. Eventually, I opted to attend sessions every other day.

My treatments were scheduled at the end of the afternoon and I would set off from Fort Kochi just as the city's schoolchildren were making their way home. They pointed and smiled at me sitting at the back of the bus. Sometimes one or two of the braver kids would approach me. 'Please sir, where are you coming from?' 'Do you like our country?' As we spoke, the rest of their classmates looked on, giggling shyly.

Arriving in Pallaruthy, I had a long walk from the bus stop to Mini's house – past stands selling fruit and snacks, as well as tiny shops in which I could see tailors, repair men, barbers and carpenters at work. From the interest I aroused, it seemed Westerners were rarely seen in these parts. Over the next couple of weeks I got to know one or two of the traders and sometimes stopped in a café for chai and halwa – a delicious, sticky sweet. On one occasion the owner presented his daughter – a beautiful young woman of about twenty. 'She has a degree you know!' he boasted, holding her in front of him like a trophy. The girl mumbled a few shy words in response to my awkward questions whilst her father looked on proudly.

On arriving at Mini's house, I'd be offered a cup of tea. Sometimes, I'd spend a few minutes with the children, who were learning English at school. Then, after my treatment with Joppen, I'd sit for a while in the house and chat with Mini. She would conclude the session by prescribing some ayurvedic medicine to take with me, and then I'd begin the long journey home.

Often, I got off the bus at the Kathakali Music Centre – a little theatre crafted in a traditional style with lots of wood and shuttered windows. Each evening featured either a concert of Indian classical music or a presentation of kathakali – the traditional Keralan style of mask theatre.

I would arrive just as the performance was getting underway, quietly taking my seat as the musicians tuned up. Each evening featured a different line-up of players – usually three musicians – with familiar instruments like tabla, sitar and violin, as well as some I'd never seen or heard, while on other nights a singer would be featured. I was mesmerised by the percussionists; listening to their complex patterns of beats and accents was like watching Time itself being dissected by a team of skilled anatomists.

The kathakali shows were very different. For an hour or so, I watched a small troupe of male actors being made-up in vivid green and orange paint and being dressed in outlandish costumes. Then, for another couple of hours, they acted out stories from the epic dramas using slow ritualistic movements. Their hands and feet turned slowly in the air while their faces twisted in wild grimaces. The hypnotic mime was accompanied by pounding drums, and by the end I felt transported to a timeless, ancient world.

Here, as in other rites and rituals I saw during my trip, something seemed to have been retained of the primal experience of Man in his Universe – a sense of the magical that has almost disappeared in the modern Western world. Mind you, I'm not sure I'd have wanted to sit through the whole drama: a traditional kathakali play can go on for several days!

After the performance had finished, the audience was invited up onto the stage to meet the actors and musicians. On my third or fourth visit I introduced myself to the compère, Sujinda (Suji). He was a big man, with an attractive boyish face, and dressed in the style of a Brahmin (member of the priestly caste) - bare-chested, wearing only a saffron-coloured lunghi (loincloth) and a holy string tied over his shoulder. I told him I was a musician and was interested in learning more about Indian music. 'Then you must visit Nagaratnama,' he said. 'She is the best singer in Kerala!'

The next morning I went to meet Suji at the Music Centre. I got on the back of his moped and we sped out of the town. The vista opened out onto a scene of rice paddies and palm trees. Canals criss-crossed the landscape. We stopped at a modest house set back from the road. An elderly woman, a little stooped, came to greet us. She was dressed in a dazzling orange sari and her eyes twinkled behind thick glasses. She led us through to a little music room that was filled with trophies and photos of her younger self in performance. Hanging on the walls were various instruments, including a couple of battered looking violins.

Suji told me where I could get a bus back to town and left. Nagaratnama smiled and pointed to a harmonium on the floor. I took my place at her feet and opened the old wooden box. I fingered a few keys and pumped the bellows tentatively. A wheezy drone rose from the instrument. We began our session intoning the OM mantra.

'Sa-ri, sa-ri, sa-ri-ga-ma, ma-ga, ma-ga, ma-ga-ri-sa.' Nagaratnama's voice glided up and down the Indian scale clear and strong while she beat out the rhythm on her thigh with the flat of her hand.

'Sa-ri, sa-ri, sa…sa…' I struggled to copy the pattern.

'Sa-ri-ga-ma!' she would shout, and back to the beginning

we'd go.

We went through these exercises for nearly an hour. The Indian method of learning music is systematic and based on repetition. There was no place for indulgent, Western self-expression here! After a few lessons, I had a basic command of some scales and patterns had even learned a few religious chants and gita (songs).

For the first time in my trip, I began to feel a bit more settled. The ayurveda treatments and music lessons were providing me with a structure. I had a routine, I was meeting people and, best of all, over the fortnight of my visits to Dr Mini, the pain around my ribs seemed gradually to have eased. I had experienced a small, but positive shift in my health – shedding a little of the anxiety, tension and fatigue that had become unwelcome companions on my journey. So why, on the very day I was to leave Kerala, did I suddenly develop a high fever?

I was used to sweating in the humid climate; now though I lay burning up on my bed in the homestay wondering what the hell was going on. Was it something I'd eaten? My body ached, I felt weak and helpless, and wondered if I should ask George if I could stay on a bit longer.

I'd developed a rough plan of making towards Pondicherry in south-east India. Other travellers had mentioned an international community there called Auroville, describing all manner of eco-projects, spiritual and cultural activities. Unfortunately, Pondicherry was on the opposite side of the country to Kerala. By public transport, Indian public transport that is, it might have taken a couple of days to get there. Besides, there were interesting places to see en route. I'd decided to head east anyway, using the southern temple-city of Madurai as a stop-off point, and had already booked a place in a sleeper compartment on a train leaving later that night.

There was no real reason to push myself, yet something

was propelling me onwards. I reasoned that I'd wait until late afternoon to see if I was fit to travel. I reassured myself the ayurvedic treatment was probably "working through". It was a "healing-crisis". Maybe I was even getting ready to leave behind in Kerala the chronic fatigue I'd lived with so many years. Such is the power of rationalization! In the event, I did feel slightly better by evening and, after a warm farewell to George and Maria, set off on foot to the ferry port.

Despite the coolness of the night, I was sweating profusely under the weight of my rucksack. I boarded the ferry, still doubtful and anxious about my decision to travel. But as soon as the boat edged away from the jetty I began to relax. There was a lively atmosphere on deck. Some young students came to talk to me and, as the vessel cut across the dark estuary under a starry sky, we stood watching the lights of Fort Kochi fade behind us – the brighter lights of Ernakulum twinkling over the water ahead.

The chugging of the ferry was a welcome distraction from my weak and aching body, and I began to feel the familiar excitement of travel displacing my worries. In Madurai, at least, I had a destination. But if I thought things would now get easier for me, I was sadly mistaken: there were even greater challenges waiting just over the horizon!

6

Lost in the Temple of Doom

At the railway station in Ernakulum, I boarded the overnight train to Madurai. I edged along the train corridor and looked for my bunk, but it was late, the carriage was dark and most of the passengers had already taken to their beds. I had resigned myself to sleeping on the floor when a guard pointed up to an empty berth in the top corner of the compartment. Dragging my luggage behind me, I hoisted myself up to the bunk and prepared to turn in.

For some reason it seemed very cold up there. Then I noticed a pair of air-conditioning outlets directly next to me. I groaned inwardly. The last thing I wanted with my fever was to get chilled in the night. Should I try to find another bunk? In the end I decided to stay where I was, and managed to block the vents with two hand-woven place mats that George had presented me as a gift when I left the homestay. Gradually the temperature in the carriage began to rise, but I didn't care; we'd all sweat if we had to!

I managed to drift into a light, dream-filled sleep accompanied by the soothing rhythm of the rattling train. Occasionally I stirred at the shrieking of steel as the wheels came to a stop at a station. Then quiet – broken only by the voices of people getting on or off the train, and the snores and occasional farts of my fellow passengers.

When I woke, dawn light was filtering through the metal blinds over the train window. I sat up and stretched. On the bunk opposite me sat an old man, already tucking into his breakfast. I was famished but had brought nothing for the journey.

The train slowed to a stop. 'Madurai?' I asked. The old man wobbled his head, smiling. I remembered that Indian headshaking and nodding could mean different things in different places. But no, we were at a small country station; it was still too early for the big city.

The peace was broken by the cries of a troupe of chai and chat (snack) sellers, hawking their wares up and down the carriages. They carried huge flasks of hot tea and baskets of freshly-baked samosas. I bought breakfast and settled back into my bunk until, a few hours later, we arrived at Madurai.

I had read about the city's magnificent temple to the fish-eyed Goddess, Minakshi, only to find the famous gopurams (pyramidal towers) under renovation and almost obscured by scaffolding and nets. Still, I had a great view from my hotel roof and spent the afternoon resting outside until the sun sank crimson over the sprawling city.

After supper, I approached the temple which was laid out like a medieval citadel with four great entrance gates. The precincts housed a giant bazaar whose stalls were filled with the usual religious paraphernalia: incense, garlands, and gaudy pictures of Hindu deities. The atmosphere was festive. Pilgrims, priests, families and tourists mingled in the marketplace – making ready for their entrance into the temple proper.

I stepped through a giant doorway, beside which a live elephant stood guard, and passed into a cool, gloomy interior. With its dark stone passageways, gigantic sculptures of mythic figures and bathing pools and shrines, the temple commanded a hushed awe. I felt like a character in a game of Dungeons and Dragons about to set off on a dangerous quest to find treasure.

Inside the temple it was less crowded, but here and there sat clusters of saddhus (holy men) praying and meditating.

Their tousled hair and painted faces gave them the look of primitive men, in touch with magical forces. For a half-hour I attached myself to an English tour group, but as I tired of the commentary, I allowed myself to drift away from the party.

Soon I was wandering alone in a labyrinth of chambers and corridors. Occasionally I'd see a devotee worshipping before some shrine or other, but mostly this part of the temple seemed empty. Lamps flickered in alcoves, illuminating elaborate wall paintings depicting gods and monsters in battle. The air was heavy with the scent of sandalwood and oil smoke. Above me, the painted ceilings swirled with hypnotic patterns.

I wandered on, deeper into the temple, with little sense of where I was going. I began to feel oppressed by the darkness and the massive stones of the walls, which seemed to bear down on me. I didn't have my watch on but figured it was no later than ten o'clock. Presumably, the place stayed open though the night; but if not, *would I get locked up here?* The idea of being left to starve in some forgotten vault of an Indian temple began to play on my mind like a malevolent shadow.

Then, from somewhere in the darkness, came a long piercing blast on an instrument. A clashing of cymbals followed. Suddenly afraid, I hid myself in a niche and waited. The noise continued, getting louder, until a procession of Brahmanic figures emerged from the gloom. There were about ten men, all bare-chested and adorned with bright face-paint; some brandished flaming torches, others held musical instruments, while the rest carried between them a large glass case containing a statue.

They stopped in the corridor, which quickly filled with fire and smoke. The glass case was set down and around it began a ritual of chanting and dancing. As I watched, I seemed to lose myself in a whirl of contorted faces, gyrating shadows and unearthly sounds. The music reached a climax of intensity, then subsided. With the religious observance now performed, the troupe moved on, seeming to dissolve into the darkness and disappearing as mysteriously as it had arrived.

As the sound of cymbals receded into silence, I wondered if I should have followed the worshippers. Instead, I stood dazed; trying to absorb what I'd just witnessed. The ritual had touched something deep, even primal, in me, but it had also seemed somehow theatrical, almost unreal. The echoes of the experience continued to reverberate inside me as I stumbled on through shadowy passageways and deserted chambers. Now I just wanted to get out.

I caught sight of something moving in the shadows ahead of me. Thin and dark and near to the ground, it was a black cat! It slowed its pace until I drew alongside. As the animal turned its eyes on me I had the eerie sensation that it was trying to communicate. "Follow me – I know the way!" it seemed to be saying. And so I did.

The cat trotted on but I kept it firmly in my sight as we hastened along corridors and through yet more deserted chambers. Soon the passageway opened onto a courtyard and I was breathing fresh air again. A starry sky hung overhead. The animal ran over to the other side of the courtyard where three elderly Indian women were sitting on the ground. They looked up and smiled as if they had been expecting me. One of them raised her arm slowly and pointed to a doorway in the wall to my right. I walked through it and found myself back in the temple precinct.

The stalls in the bazaar were closing up for the night. Around them lingered the last handfuls of devotees, still absorbed in their devotions. The surrounding shops were all shut and I walked back to my hotel in a ghostly hush.

That night I slept poorly, drifting in and out of fevered dreams. In one, I was in the back garden of my childhood home playing football. As I ran up the pitch, exhilarated, I could hear a crowd cheering and banging cymbals. All around me were strange-looking little beings – dressed in white or orange robes

– who nodded, grinned and pointed in different directions. I wondered briefly whose team I was on, but it didn't seem to matter. I kept running, intoxicated by adrenaline and the noise from the crowd. "Jon Spine! Jon Spine!" they roared.

I dribbled the ball for a few yards, and then one of the other players tackled me. I ran a bit more, got the ball again, lost it. After a while I realised I was lost. Which way was I going? Then, once again the ball was at my feet, only now I could see the goal not far ahead of me. The spectators were screaming deliriously, "Spine! Spine! Spine!" Now I was in the penalty box and had a clear view of the net. I swung my left leg back to shoot, and then...

Nothing. The dream-scene had frozen into silence. As hard as I tried, I found I couldn't move my leg. I looked down. Where the ball had been, there was now a trench in the earth; in a mound beside it was the soil that had been displaced. The football (a golden colour I now noticed) was perched on top of the mound. And now the wild cheering of the crowd turned to mocking laughter. I woke from a cacophony of jeering voices with a feeling of shame and confusion.

For some time I lay in bed pondering the dream. The golden football on the mound, the leg that wouldn't move — were they symbols of some kind? Whatever the meaning, I didn't feel encouraged or inspired by it. I also recalled the previous night's escapade in the temple, and with it, other scenes of fear and loneliness along my journey. At last, it began to dawn on me that I was developing symptoms of culture shock – something I'd read about in my guidebook but hadn't really taken seriously.

Part of the problem was that I was spending too much time on my own. I had no one to share my experiences with and no reference point for the strange events unfolding around me. I was starting to feel demotivated and depressed, and was having difficulty filling the hours of the long, hot days and warm evenings. I would wander the streets for hours on end, sketching in the marketplace, taking rickshaw rides around the town and sitting in cyber cafés writing emails home. It just didn't feel much like fun.

Finding the Gandhi Institute on the other side of town was like drawing up at an oasis after a long ride through the desert. Set in a blissfully quiet, leafy compound, the institute comprised a museum, library, study-centre and bookshop. There was even a full-size replica of the simple hut Gandhi had lived in at his ashram near Ahmedabad in Gujarat.

The place became a kind of sanctuary for me and I spent several afternoons there learning about the Mahatma or "great soul", and his pivotal role in modern Indian history. The exhibition on Gandhi's life moved me deeply – especially seeing his spectacles, sandals and stick, though I didn't want to look at the bloodstained loincloth which had been preserved from his assassination.

One day, as I sat reading at one of the large library tables, I looked up at the huge portrait of the aged Gandhi at his spinning wheel. Bald and benign, wearing nothing but a simple white dhoti (loincloth), he was pictured sitting on a low stool in front of the wheel, absorbed in the craft he advocated as a spiritual as well as political solution to India's problems. The image held me fast and, as something gave way inside me, the tears began to flow. I didn't know what I was crying about, but I knew it felt good.

As I walked out into the sunny garden, I started to feel better about life. In comparison with the suffering of Gandhi and his people, my own trials seemed trivial. A lonely Englishman going crazy in India? It wasn't the end of the world, and besides, I could always go home.

I looked up as someone came towards me on the path. It was another westerner, tall and monk-like with his shaved head and loose Indian clothes. He smiled gently as he passed me. I wondered if I should turn back and try to make contact, but when I looked round he had gone. I felt puzzled, disappointed.

But even this fleeting contact was enough for the time being. And though I didn't know it then, this single friendly glance would blossom into a connection that would be crucial later on in my journey.

I decided right away to find another ashram or community where I would have people around me to talk to – preferably other travellers. There was now a choice to be made.

Before leaving England I had been advised by a friend to seek out Shantivanam – the Forest of Peace – an ashram near the city of Tiruchirapalli (Trichy), associated with the charismatic English Benedictine monk, Bede Griffiths. At Tiruvanamalai, not far from Trichy, there was another famous ashram – this one the former home of the sage Ramana Maharshi. Both places were manageable distances by train. A third option was to go straight to the intriguing Auroville community at Pondicherry – a much longer journey.

For a couple of days I made enquiries of the two ashrams but could not get an answer from either. I thought I should probably head to Pondicherry and read up about the town's history as a former French colony. I began to relish the thought of being somewhere with a more European flavour — and it was beside the sea!

The next day, sitting in a cyber café, I looked up Auroville on the web. "The first and only internationally endorsed, ongoing experiment in human unity and transformation of consciousness…" Sounded promising. "The City of the Future — a Place for all Humanity." Could this be what I'd been looking for all along? As I was scanning and scrolling the text, I gasped. It was only a small photo, but I froze as I looked at it. It showed a giant golden globe, perched on a plinth, standing majestic against a pure blue sky. Around it were gardens and trees, dwarfed by the great orb. This was the Matrimandir, or Mother Temple, and was described as the spiritual heart of Auroville. I wondered where had I seen an image like that before.

Then I recalled the dream I'd had a few days earlier: the bizarre soccer match, the freeze-frame, the football on the mound... This temple was what I'd seen in symbolic form in my dream! I felt elated, yet frightened also. What could it all mean? I thought of the Richard Dreyfus character in the film *Close Encounters* who sees on television the image of the mountain which has been haunting him, and where the mother ship is to make contact with planet Earth. At last, I thought, a sign!

I went straight to the railway station and asked for a ticket to Pondicherry. I was told that the journey had to be made in two stages: first a train to Trichy, then a connection on to Pondicherry. For some reason there were no through tickets available so I booked a seat on the following day's midday train from Madurai to Trichy, and resigned myself to sorting out the rest of the journey from there.

I was tired of the intensity of the city and looking forward to leaving. I was also getting fed up with Indians wanting to talk to me or badgering me to take up one service or another. On my way back from the station, a small, wiry man with a tape measure around his neck sprung out from an alleyway. He stood gesticulating in front of me on the pavement.

'Good morning sir! You like nice new shirt?'

'No thank you, really...'

'Very cheap sir, good and best cloth. You come now, please sir!'

'No!' I tried to step round him.

'Ready in twenty-four hours sir, just twenty four hours!'

The tailor's pleading wore me down and, against my better judgement, I followed him up an alleyway into a small shop. Tall bolts of coloured cloth stood against the walls, overlooking a workshop where several men were bent over old-fashioned sewing machines. The whirring of treadles and rapid taktaktak of stitching filled the air.

I negotiated a price (paying half up front), chose a fabric and selected a collarless style from a range of patterns. The tailor pointed to a changing room and signalled to a younger man to come and measure me. Once inside the booth, I took off my shirt to allow the assistant to make his measurements. Somehow, as he was putting the tape round my waist, he managed to reach out and grope my balls. I jumped back.

'What the –?!' In other circumstances I might have made light of this advance, but this was surely not the time or the place. I pushed the man away and he scuttled off apologetically. Stepping back into the shop, I was unsure what to do. I wasn't so offended as to demand my money back – besides, I wanted a new shirt.

'I'll be back at eleven tomorrow morning,' I called out as I left the shop. 'And I want that shirt ready because I've got a train to catch at twelve, ok?' The tailor just wobbled his head and smiled.

I arrived the following day to find the shirt had not even been started on.

'Oh, it is no problem, sir. No problem at all!' claimed the tailor, quickly taking up his scissors and cloth. 'I am making it for you right now.'

I was livid. 'Damn right! And I'm going to stand here and watch you. I want it ready in fifteen minutes!' My imperious tone shocked me, but it had its effect. The tailor's hands became a blur as he measured and snipped. He rushed to his machine with the various sections of the shirt and I watched amazed as the pieces were stitched together and the garment began to take shape. I kept glancing at my watch: he never once looked up. With just a minute or two to spare, he proudly held up his handiwork. The shirt looked great to me, but I did not give him the satisfaction of too many thanks. I snatched it from him, slapped the balance of the payment on the counter and rushed off towards the station. I arrived, breathless and anxious, only to discover that the train to Trichy was running over an hour late.

Waiting on the platform, I realised that fatigue and loneliness were now beginning to erode my sense of common decency. I was becoming alienated from my fellow man and hardened to my environment. I was desperate for some respite from the effort of having to book accommodation, find railway and bus stations, and keep myself fed and occupied through the long and solitary days and nights.

The intriguing-sounding Auroville seemed to hold the promise of some kind of sanctuary. If only I could get there I felt I would probably be safe. Unfortunately, I had a couple of hard lessons more to learn before I would be permitted entry to the "City of the Future".

The Forest of Peace

It was four o'clock when I got off the train at Trichy and started queuing to buy my ticket on to Pondicherry. Yet even as I anticipated arriving at my seaside destination, something prompted me to try phoning the Shantivanam ashram one more time. For all I knew the place might have been just round the corner; it would be a shame not to see it if I had the chance.

Come on, I thought, pressing my mobile phone up against my ear, someone answer! I pushed my rucksack along the floor ahead of me and, just as I was about to reach the ticket counter, I got through.

'Hello, this is Shantivanam ashram. Who is speaking please?' Brother Paul was one of the junior monks at the ashram. He told me Shantivanam was only an hour away from the station and could be reached by bus. I was welcome to visit.

I jumped out of the ticket queue and set off in high spirits, refuelling with coffee and bananas en route to the bus station nearby. The journey took us out of busy Trichy, and followed a meandering route alongside the sacred Cauvery River. Somehow, despite passing through beautiful, fertile-looking country, I could feel my mood of optimism and good fortune slowly dissolving. Should I have so readily abandoned my plan to go straight to Pondicherry? Why had I followed this whim of an idea to visit a place I knew next to nothing about?

I reassured myself that the delay would probably be no more

than a couple of days and besides, the experience might be very rewarding. An established spiritual community that had been the home of a saintly Englishman had to be worth seeing.

Following the monk's instructions, I got off the bus in the nearest settlement to the ashram – a sleepy village of thatched mud huts clustered round a dusty square. It was almost dark now and I was tired. I looked anxiously for a rickshaw to take me the few kilometres back along the main road to Shantivanam. All I saw was a handful of men standing outside their huts, the lit ends of their beedis glowing in the gloom.

Soon, a sullen-faced old man came towards me wheeling a bicycle rickshaw. I asked him the price of the journey. He barked an answer and started blustering me towards his vehicle. With some apprehension I got in and watched as his sinewy legs strained to get the rickshaw moving. But there was something wrong with the bike and, as we lurched along the potholed road, I became impatient at our slow progress. At one point we were overtaken by two young schoolgirls on their bicycles – causing my driver to spit and grumble.

At last, we arrived at the slope leading from the main road up to the ashram. After a few more tortuous yards, the rickshaw came to a stop. I jumped out and started pushing from the back to help the driver get moving again, but he obviously didn't want to go any further.

'You walk now,' he said, pointing to the ashram gate some way ahead on the track. Something in his tone made me angry.

'You keep going!' I shouted, shocked by my own defiance.

I got back in the rickshaw and waited. Raising a string of curses as he strained his muscles, the driver heaved the vehicle forwards and we trundled painfully up to the gate. I got down and paid him what we'd agreed. He counted the cash and started babbling angrily at me, pushing his hands forward as if to demand more. I was sure I'd paid the correct amount. Did he really expect me to tip him?

In any other situation I would have given extra, but there

was something about this driver that I didn't like. No matter that I had a pocketful of money and he was a poor man; I wasn't going to be bullied into paying over the odds for such a lousy service.

I grabbed my rucksack and entered the ashram in a temper. Then I noticed a robed figure, presumably the gatekeeper, sitting just inside the compound. He must have witnessed the whole exchange and I instantly felt ashamed at bringing my anger into a spiritual space.

Nor did things get any better. There was no one in the ashram office to greet me, and when, after a long wait in the reception, I was finally attended to, it was by a middle-aged American woman who was irritatingly vague. 'I'm not sure we've got much room at the moment,' she said dreamily.

'But the monk said – '

'Oh well, the monks don't always know, I'm afraid. Let's see now, we might have some space. Perhaps I should go and find out. Can you wait for a bit?'

Eventually, I was accommodated in a monastic "cell", with a hard bed, a desk, a little shelf space, and an overhead fan – useful against the mosquitoes which were prolific here. Venturing out, I found the toilet and shower blocks and the main ashram buildings: kitchen, dining hall and chapel.

Shantivanam was smaller than I'd imagined and seemed more like a little forest village than a religious retreat. Simple huts nestled between huge palmyra trees and, in one corner, a new temple was under construction. Everywhere I went, the atmosphere was subdued and contemplative.

Only a handful of Indian Benedictine monks – distinctive in their long brown robes – remained in the resident community. Despite the presence of numerous other guests, including foreign visitors like myself, and an assortment of visiting priests, a curious sense of desertedness seemed to hang about the place.

For a day or two I tried to join in the routine of worship

which was based around the Catholic mass, but with a strong Hindu flavour. I sang psalms in English and hymns in Tamil (the state language). Fascinating stuff, but what was a Jewish Buddhist doing praying to Jesus and having sacred ash and sandalwood smeared on his forehead?

Mealtimes were austere in the extreme. Two long mats ran the length of the dining-hall where we sat on the floor, facing one another in silence. At the sound of a bell, a monk came round ladling out idli and sambar (a thin lentil and vegetable stew) onto our metal trays. A dish of curd and a glass of water completed the meal. For me, the experience was joyless. I tried to imagine the charismatic Bede Griffiths amongst us; surely he would not have begrudged his guests a smile?

I knew little about the great man who'd lived here from 1968 until his death in 1993, other than the fact that he'd played a pivotal role in the development of contemplative Christianity in India. Later, I learned of Griffiths' conventional English upbringing, the epiphany he had whilst at school, subsequent education at Oxford, and his taking of Benedictine vows at Prinknash Abbey. It seemed he became disillusioned with the state of English monasticism and made his way to India in 1955. After a number of attempts to live in religious communities, he arrived at the ashram at Trichy, originally founded by two French monks, and then known as Saccidananda (a Hindu word meaning "being, consciousness, bliss").

Griffiths began to grow the Shantivanam community and, over the next 25 years, evolved a synthesis of Catholicism and Hinduism that attracted devotees from around the world. Renegade Indian nuns and priests apparently found in Griffiths a living example of the true Christian spirit: humble yet determined, radical yet accommodating, fearless yet forgiving. He was also known and loved by the ordinary Indian villagers for miles around. Here though, in my state of depletion and irritation, I could sense nothing of this great man's legacy, and soon started wondering why I had bothered to come at all.

My mood improved a little when Ram Dass Shennoy arrived. A gangly character in his sixties, with a mischievous face surrounded by greying hair and a patchy beard, this middle-aged Goan described himself as a "pukka ashram fellow". He moved into the room next to mine and we got to know each other as we took walks around the compound and on the banks of the Cauvery, a stone's throw away.

Ram Dass explained to me how he had left his householder's life behind him and taken to the roads of India in the tradition of the sanyassi (one who has renounced the world). He told me that he had then got involved in running an ashram himself. It seemed he had left under mysterious circumstances – financial trouble, probably. From time to time he would produce from his pocket a clutch of tatty, folded papers which he claimed gave him legal right to some property or other. There would follow improbable stories of threats and kidnappings, which he'd escaped only by divine intervention.

'Jon,' he would say with a portentous look, 'God is good, God is good!' Pausing for a moment and fixing me with a look over the top of his glasses, he'd add: 'So Jon, what is your opinion of this matter?' Then, without waiting for an answer, he'd go on to relate yet another outlandish incident from the spiritual marketplace of southern India. I took all this in half-seriously, glad to have any company at all.

Then I really fell ill. I suspected something was wrong when I began to loathe the sight of the food I was being served. I had, on my trip, already eaten enough idli and sambar to last a lifetime, but there was nothing else on offer here. What began as a routine dose of the runs escalated into something more serious and soon I was stranded in my room, unable to eat and barely drinking. I went out only to dash to the toilet where my poor body tried vainly to expel whatever was ailing it. I felt horribly nauseous, alone and uncared for.

In the stifling heat and darkness of my shuttered room, I was dehydrating fast. By now I had lost all track of time and was beginning to lose my bearings too. I felt utterly disconnected from my surroundings and all human warmth. Over the partition wall between our rooms, I could hear Ram Dass chanting mantras – his drone punctuated by fits of hawking and spitting. The monotonous whirring of the fan seemed impossibly loud: the only variation in the sound was the short, insistent buzzing of mosquitoes coming to feed on me.

At some point, one of the other foreign visitors knocked on the door and asked if I was alright. I told her I was very sick and didn't know what to do. A short while later Brother Martin, the most senior monk, arrived with the ashram administrator and decided I ought to be taken to hospital immediately. Minutes later, two junior Indian monks were driving me in a Land Rover to Trichy where I was admitted to the Child Jesus Infirmary – a large public hospital in the city.

I stumbled in, supported by Brother Peter and Brother Paul. A wheelchair was found for me and I was parked in a long, high-ceilinged corridor waiting to begin the admission process. Lining the corridor was a multitude of Indian women and children, some sitting still and anxious in their seats, others more animated. One little boy, dressed only in tattered orange shorts, pointed at me, giggling shyly. I managed to smile back.

I began to feel better simply being amongst ordinary people, and took comfort in the hospital activity, uniforms and equipment around me. I chatted with the monks as we waited and learned something of their lives as Indian monastics. They shared reminiscences of Bede Griffiths, who they obviously adored, and I came to understand something of the grief the community still felt in his absence.

At last I was taken onto the ward and put on a drip feed. I could actually feel the life seeping back into me as the rehydration fluid worked its wonders. I was also started on a course of antibiotics to deal with any gastric infection I may have had.

For three blissful days I lay in a clean, comfortable bed and was fussed over by a team of pretty young Indian nurses. How graceful and attentive they were! They moved slowly and deliberately in an atmosphere of faith and devotion, not unlike nuns. Around the ward, stylized posters of an immaculately groomed blonde Jesus beamed down from the walls, bearing mottoes like "We put on the bandages, God does the healing".

I wondered about this conjunction of religion and medicine – something most people in the West would now consider archaic, controversial even. Here in India though, it seemed to make perfect sense; after all, without some reverence towards the body, mind and spirit, what is medicine really doing? I went along with it all, even allowing some earnest Christian pastors to pray over me on my last evening.

On being discharged, I returned to Shantivanam feeling a whole lot better. Though I wanted to move on as soon as possible to Pondy, I was determined to see if I could connect with the spirit of the ashram before leaving. Perhaps I needed to be a little more proactive?

I asked if I could use the library – an octagonal, timber building near the centre of the community. Inside was a superb collection of spiritual and literary books in various languages. I also requested permission to enter the modest hut where Bede Griffiths himself had lived. Here I sat quietly, trying to imagine the life of the sage who had slept, worked and prayed here. I felt calm and peaceful, but couldn't shake off the vague feeling of sadness and absence that lingered over the place.

I also began talking to some of the other visitors and noticed a friendly, familiar-looking face among the small group of international guests. I smiled and walked over to the tall, shaven-headed man.

'Have we met?' I asked.

'I'm not sure, have we?'

'Only, your face looks familiar.' Then I remembered. 'Were

you at the Gandhi Museum in Madurai recently?'

He laughed and said he had noticed me there too. He introduced himself as Adrian, from London, and told me he was travelling around India, visiting ashrams and doing yoga and meditation. He'd spent some years training as a Buddhist monk in Burma, but was now living back in the UK and feeling a bit lost. He said he was planning to stay at Shantivanam a couple of days longer and then move on, also to Pondy. We swapped numbers and I hoped we would see one another again.

In the meantime, Ram Dass Shennoy had decided that he was going to throw himself on the mercy of the famous Aurobindo ashram at Pondicherry, and so we agreed to travel together. The following morning we left Shantivanam, taking a lift with an Indian priest to the railway station at Trichy. From here we caught the train to Pondicherry – a journey of several hours.

It wasn't an altogether comfortable trip. With his interminable prattle, Ram Dass could be tiring company. The story of his escapades in ashrams throughout India had now assumed epic proportions: kidnappings and ransoms were followed by miracles and divine revelations; a near-fatal stabbing had made the national papers; one of his gurus had embezzled an organisation and been buried alive... Each new twist in the plot would culminate in Ram Dass' magical deliverance, and be concluded with the refrain, "So Jon, what is your opinion of this matter?"

Then there was the issue of money. As an "ashram fellow", Ram Dass was travelling, so he said, with very little money. I was a Western tourist, doing India on a credit card. Now, travelling with an Indian companion, I wasn't sure how far my financial responsibility should extend. I was happy to treat him to chai, coffee and snacks during the journey; whenever I bought from the vendors on the train, Ram Dass would happily take his portion, grin and say, "God is good. Oh yes Jon, God is good!" Of course He's good, I thought privately, when it's me that's paying!

Even though the sums of money involved were tiny, there was something uncomfortable about always being the provider. It would have been far worse however to have bought for myself and not shared. I decided that I was, in essence, paying Ram Dass for his company and local knowledge. There are certainly worse reasons to give.

In the lulls between Ram Dass's outlandish tales, I had some moments to reflect on where I'd got to in my "Indian Odyssey". Out of England for two months now, I felt I had had more than enough adventure. I was weary and looked forward to recuperating by the sea. I imagined Pondicherry might be my last stop in south India and wanted, more than anything, to get to Auroville. If I could only get a bit stronger, maybe I could spend a while there, volunteering perhaps. Hadn't I, after all, had a dream, a sign, and been called to the Matrimandir?

Fate was, indeed, to grant me my wish – but in a most cruel and dramatic way.

Pondicherry

A balmy, humid evening greeted us as Ram Dass and I got out of the train at Pondicherry. We walked from the station towards the seafront and found a room at the Park Guest Hotel, a grand apartment complex on the beach. The place was part of a network of properties and businesses owned by the Aurobindo organisation – named after the guru, Sri Aurobindo, whose influence lies behind the Auroville community.

From the outset there was no mistaking that we were in a "spiritual" hotel. All around were posters advising prudence and mindfulness, and there was a barrage of rules and regulations as to appropriate conduct on the premises: "Any display of swimwear is prohibited." "Guests permitted in the dining room between 4 and 5pm ONLY." But the accommodation at least was comfortable, reasonably priced and overlooking the sea.

When Ram Dass and I went out for a walk along the seafront, I was instantly enchanted. Stretching ahead of us was a long promenade dotted with ice-cream stalls and vendors of snacks and drinks. I could see a smart beachside café and palm trees, while guest houses and hotels lined the other side of the street. Indians and foreigners strolled casually along in the cool evening, accompanied by the sound of waves crashing on the rocky beach beside us. The sky went through a vivid watercolour display of yellows, pinks and reds before night closed in and we headed home.

The following morning, Ram Dass went off to register with the Aurobindo authorities, claiming that as a sanyassi he was eligible for free board and lodgings at any ashram in India. From the little experience I had gained of ashrams, I was not very hopeful for him. Sure enough, he returned later, disconsolate, with the news that here his status as an "ashram fellow" was not being honoured. Unable himself to afford to stay at the hotel, and sensing (quite rightly) that my generosity would not extend to subsidising his entire visit, he decided to head back to Tiruvanamalai and try his luck at Ramana Maharshi's ashram.

On parting, we hugged and exchanged gifts. He gave me an attractive wooden mala (Indian rosary beads), and I gave him a scarlet lunghi (wraparound skirt worn by men) I'd bought in Madurai but had not yet felt brave enough to wear. I watched Ram Dass walk off towards the station and wondered what further incredible adventures lay in store for him. Once again, I was on my own.

I took advantage of my solitude to rest thoroughly and indulge myself in this European-style resort town. There were good restaurants to eat in, and Western-style supermarkets where I bought tins of tuna, rice cakes and other foods that gave me a semblance of being in my normal life. I had coffee and cake in the expensive beachside café; I sketched and painted by the sea and wandered the wide, leafy streets in the French quarter with their craft boutiques, galleries and bookshops.

At the Pondicherry museum I learned that the settlement dated back to the seventeenth century, when the French established a base there. By 1750 French power in India was at its peak; Pondy was the main port and administrative centre – prosperous enough to rival Madras, then in the hands of the British. Only in 1952, when the Franco-Indian colonial empire was liquidated, had Pondy and other French possessions been ceded to India.

It was the arrival in 1910 of the Indian sage and mystic, Sri Aurobindo, which really made Pondicherry. Though he died in 1950, the influence of this unique figure, as well as his consort – known simply as "the Mother" – was unmistakable. Streets, buildings and businesses were named after the two of them, and one could see, at any time of day or night, little groups of devotees making their way to or from the ashram in the heart of the city.

Early in my stay I went to visit the ashram, not really sure what I would find there. It was late afternoon, and still very warm, as I waited amongst a large crowd in the street outside the gates. There seemed to be a lot of middle-aged Western women, most in Indian dress, and serious-looking Indian men in neat, short-sleeved shirts and slacks. The mood was calm but anticipatory.

On a signal, the gates opened and we filed silently into a courtyard decked with flowers. Garlands and wreathes were stacked in an enormous floral display around an imposing stone sepulchre. This was the samadhi (resting-place) of Aurobindo and the Mother. I could sense it was a site of tremendous significance for those who already sat praying or meditating – several were quietly weeping – but the experience left me unmoved.

I needed to know something of the background to what was unfolding around me. Fortunately, the hotel where I was staying had a small library and study room containing the collected works of Aurobindo and the Mother. Here I got a flavour of the sage's visionary thought (and elevated prose style), as well as the Mother's more practical advice to their followers.

The next evening, I went back to the ashram with some questions. An assistant suggested I attend a meditation in the "playground" – the open-air courtyard in the ashram school nearby. Within about fifteen minutes, a hundred or more of us had gathered under the stars, taking our places around the edges of the sports ground. We had to wait until the previous activity – a fitness class for elderly ashramites – had finished. A dozen or so pensioners were being led in a military-style exercise routine by a short, stocky man in khaki, barking instructions in French. The members of his unlikely platoon were dressed identically in white shirts, shorts, socks and plimsolls. They hopped, skipped and jumped cautiously through their drill and, when they reached one or other end of the tarmac, the instructor would blast on a whistle and the whole party would shuffle round and head back the other way. It could have come straight out of Monty Python.

At last, the space was cleared for meditation. The crowd now dispersed over the whole playground; each person finding a space to sit and prepare for what was to follow. I imagined perhaps a half-hour of silent communing, and settled, as well as I was able, into a half-lotus posture on the hard floor.

My reverie was shattered by a ghostly voice ringing out overhead. 'If your power of concentration is complete, then there is not a problem you cannot solve…'

The voice belonged to a woman; the words were delivered slowly, in a thickly accented English, made more difficult to understand by boomy amplification. There was a quavering tone to the speech that suggested mystical absorption, like a medium in trance. At the same time, a projection appeared, high on the opposite wall, of the Mother's face – already familiar to me from the posters and photos all around the town. Thick, greying hair was pulled tightly back from an ageing face whose features expressed a curious mixture of severity and softness. Her eyes, in particular, seemed at once stern and kind: even from the image, I could sense the charismatic power of the Mother's gaze.

The recorded speech was followed by a few minutes of unfamiliar organ music, whose distant, reedy tone evoked other worlds. In the following silence I tried to settle myself into meditation, but couldn't quite shake off the associations with seventies sci-fi and the "Hammer House of Horror".

The following morning, I spotted Adrian standing at a chai stall in the town. We sat together on the corner, drinking and chatting. He was in good spirits and I asked him how he had managed to adapt so easily to the solo traveller's life in India. He told me this was not his first time here: he had a little network of contacts around the country and was following a loose itinerary. On top of that, his mother was flying over shortly from the UK to visit him in Pondy. He said he'd probably be busy for a few days but that I should ring if I needed anything.

Buoyed up by the encounter, I decided actively to seek out some company. I went to a backpackers' café and got talking to some Brits who were partying their way around India. Later, I went to see an art exhibition at the Alliance Française cultural centre and struck up conversation with a friendly young man, Mr. Kathir, who turned out to be a Tamil chess champion. He introduced me in turn to his friend, Mr. Perisswamy, who was keen to practise his English with me. Now I had a few people to talk to and places to visit; it seemed my fortunes were on the up, and I began to feel more confident and hopeful.

Then came my first opportunity to visit Auroville. I hired a rickshaw and driver and was dropped off at the entrance to the "City of the Future" – actually a collection of villages, projects and building developments spread over a rural area about ten kilometres north of Pondicherry. In contrast with the garish disarray of the typical Indian street-scene, everything here looked neat and clean. The buildings were stylish, the gardens carefully tended, and the people well dressed. In Auroville, it seemed, the benign chaos of India had been tamed by efficient European organisation.

At the visitor centre, I watched a video explaining and celebrating the history of the community. I then joined a group of middle-class Indian tourists (to judge from their well-pressed clothes, designer spectacles and jewellery), and was led on a walk through dusty, tree-shaded lanes to see the edifice which, we were told, represented the "spiritual heart of Auroville". I had dreamed of it, I had seen a picture of it; now I was going to stand in the presence of the mighty Matrimandir.

The woodland path along which we were walking opened out onto a spit of land overlooking a wide grassy plain. Ahead of us, glowing in the light of the intense afternoon sun, stood an enormous golden sphere, perhaps a hundred feet high. Gazing at the massive orb, I felt I had stepped into the landscape of a future civilization. As my eye scanned the stippled surface of the structure – which looked a bit like a giant golf ball, squashed at the top – I felt a thrill of recognition, almost déjà vu. This was what I had dreamed of, and then seen on the internet. But why this place? And what had it to do with me?

Unfortunately, the group was not allowed into the temple. There was a complicated system for booking visits and this time, at least, I had to be content with this tantalizing view of the exterior. I resolved to come back as soon as I could.

Back in Pondicherry, I was becoming anxious about my accommodation. The staff at the Park Guest Hotel would only allow me to book one day ahead. Apparently, the anniversary of the Mother's birthday was approaching and they were expecting a lot more visitors – mostly devotees with a greater claim on available beds. It wasn't a satisfactory situation for me, but it did at least clarify that I should now try to relocate to Auroville.

I quickly found out that most of the facilities for tourists and visitors in the City of the Future were either full, or expensive. I got a couple of leads from other travellers for places that would accept volunteers – with bed and board (often very basic) offered in return for a number of hours work each day. But I wondered if I was physically up to the demands of the more agricultural and ecological projects.

The only thing to do was to go in person and see if I could find somewhere that would accept me. The two projects I particularly wanted to see were Buddha's Garden and Saddhana Forest – both of which were exploring sustainable agriculture and running volunteer programmes. I would explain my situation and ask if I could stay a couple of weeks. But first I had to get there.

Auroville sprawls over an area of about twenty square kilometres and most people use mopeds or bikes to get around. I'd never ridden a motor scooter before and was hesitant about hiring one in India, of all places. For a day or two I wrestled with the idea, finally deciding if I wanted to explore Auroville I would have to take the risk.

I'd got to know one of the security guards at the hotel who said he could rent me a scooter cheaply. I insisted he bring me a helmet as well – despite the fact that almost nobody in India wears one. I told him I had insurance and was reassured that a driving license was all the documentation I needed.

The following Sunday morning (it was the 12th of February), I took the keys to a sturdy Vespa-style bike, along with a crash helmet. After a brief test drive outside the hotel, I set off along the beach road, nervous and excited. A flawless cobalt sky stretched overhead while the sun caressed everything with its warmth. Dressed only in a T-shirt, shorts and sandals, I was experiencing the intoxicating freedom of being abroad, whizzing along on a bike with the wind on my face and a whole day ahead to explore.

I thought I'd chosen a quiet time for my maiden voyage, but there seemed to be just as many lorries, buses, rickshaws, bicycles, pedestrians and animals on the road as ever. Everything was in motion, moving at different speeds in different directions. I marvelled at the apparent ease with which other drivers weaved in and out across the whole roadway – overtaking here, undertaking there. My ears were filled with the roar of engines, hooters and radios, shouts and fragments of conversation. Lorries and buses thundered past me, decorated with wildly coloured designs and hand-painted lettering. The dazzling pinks and brilliant greens of saris flashed by as women passed on the back of motorcycles – scarves of loose cloth flapping dangerously behind them. And a swarm of rickshaws, with their distinctive black and yellow livery, buzzed like angry wasps through the general insanity, belching acrid blue diesel smoke.

Despite all this distraction, I was getting more comfortable on my scooter, and the journey out of Pondy passed without incident. As I approached Auroville on the main East Coast Road, the traffic became lighter until, miraculously, I seemed to have the road all to myself. I thought I knew where I was supposed to turn off the main road, but I somehow missed it. No matter, at the next petrol station I bought fuel for the bike and headed back the way I'd come. Now I saw the Auroville turning on my right but this time overshot it. I looked around me, saw nothing coming, then started to U-turn in the road. Out of the corner of my eye, I sensed something rushing towards me in the opposite lane. There was no time to react. In the next moment, an angry red motorbike came roaring into my right side. Instinctively, I threw out my left leg to try and steady the scooter but it couldn't bear the force. The action seemed to unfold frame by frame as I keeled over, bike on top of me. As I hit the road, I had the curious experience of not feeling altogether surprised at what was happening. What a drag, I thought to myself with resignation, I'm having an accident.

For the next few moments I lay absolutely still on the ground, trying to take in what had happened. At first I felt only the road-burn where my bare skin had made contact with the asphalt. Then I realised my body somehow didn't feel like me anymore: I wondered which limbs I could still move. The right arm and left leg in particular seemed to have turned to jelly. Slowly, the reality of the situation began to dawn on me and with it came the pain proper. The slightest movement sent shocking, burning waves through my body. Now I knew I was really in trouble.

Fortunately, I'd come off not far from a parade of shops and a rickshaw rank. A small crowd of Indians began to assemble; peering down at me, discussing what should be done. I looked up into the circle of strange faces. 'Please!' I moaned, 'Please, someone call a doctor!'

'No doctor coming here!' came the reply.

Someone managed to move the scooter off and away from me; another got my water bottle out of my bag and helped me drink. Bizarrely, I remember wanting to wash clean some of the raw patches on my limbs – as if this would remedy the situation.

'Can you get me to a hospital?' I pleaded.

Two men tried to lift and support me between them, but as I attempted to walk, my legs crumpled beneath me. I cried out in agony as they lay me down on the pavement. A furious jabbering started up as people argued over what to do. I felt hot and sick and close to passing out. Then a dark, solid figure emerged from the crowd and seemed to take charge. 'I know good hospital,' the man said, 'we go now!' Gently he lifted me into the back of his rickshaw and set off along the East Coast Road.

'My name Vasu!' he shouted back to me over the engine noise. I could see his concerned eyes in the rear-view mirror. In between my moans I told him my name and where I was staying.

'You money, Jon?'

'Yes Vasu, I've got money. Please, just get me to the hospital quickly!' I sat at a twisted angle in the rickshaw, holding on to the sidebar with my good arm and bracing myself against each excruciating jolt in the pot-holed road.

'I sorry Jon, I sorry!' Vasu called out in response to my cries.

By now, I had become aware of a new sensation: a dull

vibration in the core of my being which threatened to grow, spread and engulf me. I guessed this must be shock kicking in and, while I didn't think I was going to die, I began to be scared.

I tried to focus on the scenery rushing past. On our right, between us and the beach, lay the broken villages that had been battered by the devastating tsunami of 2004. On the left was open land, scattered with isolated houses, shops, and buildings belonging to the University of Pondicherry. Everywhere, people were going about their business, oblivious to the drama unfolding in my life.

Eventually, Vasu swung off the main road onto a peaceful country lane winding through palm forest. At a sign for the "Pondicherry Institute of Medical Science" (PIMS), we passed between huge iron gates and onto a spacious estate. Ahead of us stood a complex of modern white buildings set in parkland. We sped past trees, flowers and well-tended lawns and pulled up at Accident and Emergency. Whilst I could register every detail of the scene, it all seemed unreal.

Within seconds, hospital staff had surrounded the rickshaw. Two men manoeuvred me out of the vehicle and lay me on a stretcher trolley. As I was wheeled into the building, I looked up into the sympathetic faces hovering over me. My consciousness had narrowed into a sharp beam, focused on my physical survival. Along with the trembling feelings of shock and the searing pain that came with even the slightest movement of my limbs, I felt an intense need for contact. *Please,* I thought, *talk to me, touch me, smile at me!* Waves of loneliness and dread swelled over me and I sank into darkness.

The English Patient

'Mr Stein, can you hear me?' The voice was distant and muffled, reaching me as if through water. I opened my eyes and saw the kind face of a man. I nodded at him, unable yet to find any words.

'My name is Doctor Poduval. I am in charge of the team that will be looking after you.'

I tried to smile at him.

'You are going to be alright, Mr Stein. Now, do you have anybody with you?'

I felt someone put a hand reassuringly on my shoulder. It was Vasu. Then came more questions: name, address, next of kin. I gasped out my answers as, once again, I began to become aware of the pain cutting through my body. My bloodied shorts were cut off of me, my blood pressure was taken, and my leg and arm were prodded.

'Does this hurt?'

'And what about this?'

'Yes, yes!' I couldn't help myself shouting. 'That bloody well hurts!'

Various other doctors introduced themselves and one of them told me X-rays would have to be taken and I'd probably need surgery. For now though, there were injections, a drip-feed, thermometers; I was only half-aware of what was going on. As I was wheeled along the open-air walkways linking various hospital departments, I was struck by the intense blueness of the sky above. *Please!* I prayed, please, *just let me enjoy this world again!* Exactly who or what I was appealing to was not clear to me.

I was taken to a consulting room where I was asked yet more questions. Did I want a private room? Inspired by Gandhi's example of being "at one with the people" (and with more than a hint of self-martyrdom), I refused. I soon found myself lying in an enormous general ward filled with Indian patients, most of whom seemed to have their entire families in attendance – tucking into food, watching television or even sleeping on the floor. The overhead fan whirred above me like a rescue helicopter. Only, there was to be no rescue.

After an hour's groaning misery on my bed, and unable even to get the attention of a nurse, I knew I would not last much longer in this environment. That question I'd been asked on arrival about having anybody with me, revealed an important assumption about healthcare in Indian hospitals, where patients are often admitted in the company of family members who may feed and even nurse them. Whilst Vasu was willing to help as much as he could, he and I could not communicate with much fluency. I badly needed someone to advocate for me – but who?

I still had my mobile phone with me. Luckily, it was charged and there was a signal. I called Adrian in Pondy, explained to him what had happened and begged him to come quickly to the hospital. Half an hour later he arrived, signed some paperwork and managed to negotiate my move to a private room. My scruples would simply have to wait.

I learned from yet another doctor that I'd suffered a "tibial condyle fracture" of the left leg, and a "radial neck fracture" of the right arm. Basically, the arm should heal without surgery but the leg was much more serious. Under the impact of my collision with the motorbike, he explained, the femur (upper leg bone) had been forced downwards, puncturing the top of the tibia (lower leg bone), which had fractured badly and would need two or three metal pins to fix it.

An "elevation and percutaneous screw fixation" may sound like a sexual perversion, but it is apparently a fairly routine operation. I would be going into theatre early the following morning. Naturally, I was nervous, and the disclaimer I signed, acknowledging the potentially fatal effects of anaesthesia, did not reassure me. But at least I had remembered to revise my will before leaving the UK.

I was helped to sleep that night by a Valium 10 that Adrian had miraculously produced from his wallet before leaving the hospital. For some reason, the PIMS staff seemed reluctant to give me pain relief: perhaps it was part of the ethos of spiritual healing that persisted here alongside a more Western approach.

I remember going into theatre and the beginning of the operation, but then I must have drifted off. The last thing I remember was gazing into a pair of deep brown eyes. A doctor? A nurse? It didn't matter. In them, I saw an ocean of calm and peace that seemed to wash my fear away.

When I woke, I was told everything had gone well. A wave of relief and gratitude flooded over me. I've made it, I thought, I've come through! And though still groggy, I almost enjoyed the wheelchair ride up to the room on Special Ward One, which was to be my home for the next three-and-a-half weeks.

Room 52 was long and narrow with a high ceiling. On the right stood a high bed, neatly made up with crisp sheets; at the far end was a window and a small bathroom. I also had a television, a cupboard to store my things, and a second, low bed which visitors could use as a couch. Everything was painted the same dull yellow colour and the space was devoid of decoration or ornament, but I knew how lucky I was to be in such a clean and quiet environment.

Only it wasn't so quiet. I quickly learned that my recovery was not to be such a private process. In fact, I had to get used to being public property, and for the door of my room to open at any time to admit nurses, doctors and other personnel.

The day began around five o'clock in the morning with a bed bath. Still half-asleep, I had no choice but to relax as the burly male nurse, Murugan, bustled into the room, flicked the light on, and proceeded to strip the bed, then me. A tacit relationship of sympathy developed between us as each day he gently sponged my limbs and face and dressed me in clean hospital pyjamas. Freshly washed and changed, I fell back to dozing through the dawn – a little child again.

Then came the nurses, clean-smelling and efficient in their starched white uniforms, to check my temperature and blood-pressure and give me my medication. I soon discovered which of them liked to chat, which to laugh, and which to simply get on with their job. Next to arrive were the cleaners who spent a while sweeping and mopping the room.

There were doctors' rounds in the late morning and late afternoon. These could be quite jolly, as I seemed to have at least three doctors supervising my case. With them usually was a handful of medical students and sometimes even a nurse or two. Sprinkled in with the medical talk would be some comments or questions about life in England – about which they were intensely curious. Dr Poduval had trained in Manchester and was surprised to learn that I, too, had studied there – albeit briefly.

During the day there were several more nurses' calls, as well as the regular delivery of meals and refreshments by several different women. One of these, a bold Bengali named Lata, seemed to take a special interest in my recovery. She was short and stocky with the face of a mischievous schoolgirl. Sometimes, after putting down my food tray, she would linger and shyly try out a word or two of English. From her I learned the Hindi word "dost" (friend). One day she came in as I was watching some daytime rubbish on TV. She took the remote from me, flicked through the channels until a Bollywood film appeared, then sat down to watch.

Whether it was a particularly steamy movie, or I was just a little susceptible to Lata's strong feminine presence I don't know, but as I lay there and watched the high-energy dance routines, I started to become aroused. All the characters on the screen were fully dressed, and there was little physical contact between them, yet they conveyed a sexuality much more enticing than the no-holds-barred pornography of the West. I looked over to Lata. She sat with a sly smile on her face, absorbed in the show. I was feeling a strange mixture of excitement and anxiety; Lata must have sensed that I was embarrassed and soon left to get back to work, her laughter trailing behind her.

On another occasion a young male nurse, Murali, came to change my dressings. His dark skin and smooth hair were immaculate. He leaned in close to me and I breathed his clean soapy smell. As he worked, he tried to explain something of the cult of the Shiva lingam which I knew was linked with fertility worship. I suspected there might have been some phallic significance to the little black stone he showed me before he left, and wondered if he had been making some kind of tentative advance. But I was not as receptive as I might have been to such contact: the idea of the body as a source of pleasure, let alone sexuality as a route to enlightenment, was very far from my thoughts.

Over the course of this journey, illness and injury had shattered my confidence in my body – already dented through the negative experiences of the previous decade. I was shocked to find myself now taking some masochistic pleasure in my suffering. Could there be spiritual merit in the endurance of physical pain?

The idea of being chosen to suffer is dangerous but alluring, and here was a chance to take on the role in a more public way. Gaunt and shaven-headed, quiet and tearful, I lay on display with Gandhi's autobiography like a Bible at my bedside. And slowly the visitors started to arrive.

I met administrators of various seniority up to vice-president of the hospital trust, staff from physiotherapy and occupational health, a psychologist, several fellow patients, as well as those wanting to read to me from the real Bible, play chess, or simply practise their English.

Naturally, I played to the gallery. As the sightseers filed in, I would turn my head to look on each in turn, extending my left hand (the only one I could move) to the men, and smiling gently at the women. I'd drop in a few words here and there about my gratitude towards India and its people. This one wanted an autograph, that one a photo. Soon though, the novelty of celebrity began to pall, and I had to draw the line when some giggly student nurses turned up with no other purpose it seemed than to be able to say that they too had seen the "English Patient".

There were also some welcome personal visitors; though sadly, not Adrian – he had set off for northern India. Vasu came several times each week, often bringing little treats or supplies: paper and pens, nuts and fruit. On one occasion, he even smuggled in a couple of takeaway pizzas and cans of beer. Another time he brought his wife and three children who sat shyly and quietly on the low bed, stealing glances at the mysterious foreigner. Minutes passed in awkward silence, but I managed to break the ice by drawing pictures with the youngsters.

Grateful as I was for the company of the man who had "saved" me, I was also a little concerned about our developing relationship. Naturally I would reimburse Vasu for whatever he brought me, and add some money for the petrol he was using driving back and forth to the hospital (I was also conscious of the time he was spending away from his work). If he came around a mealtime, I'd order another portion of biryani and we'd eat together, usually watching cricket on TV. It felt good to relax in company but it was sometimes hard to get Vasu to leave. There was a touch of the master/servant dynamic that was uncomfortable for me, but I hope there was enough genuine fellow feeling to balance the emotional and economic dependency that could have arisen in the situation.

It seemed the news of my accident was now spreading beyond the hospital. One day Vasu arrived with a stout, middle-aged German woman who introduced herself as Irmgard. She told me she lived on the edge of Auroville, had heard about me, and wondered if I needed any help. She was a forceful woman, fiercely independent and seemingly critical of nearly everyone and everything in India, yet we struck up a curious friendship. She took on a motherly role, bringing me books and flowers and generally making my hospital room a bit more homely.

I listened patiently to Irmgard's tales of her life and adventures. She had married young, and unhappily. After her children had grown, she yearned for adventure and began to travel independently, visiting communities around the world. She had read a magazine article about Auroville, described as the "freest place on Earth", and had come to visit. Fifteen years later, she still hadn't left.

Then there were the Tamil guys I had met at the Alliance Française in Pondy: Mr Kathir, who came and thrashed me at chess, and Mr Perisswamy, who conjugated his English verbs by my bedside. To them, I was always "Mr Jon". I don't know why we retained the formal titles, but it seemed respectful and friendly, if slightly comical.

"Good morning, Stein, time for a little exercise!" These words announced the arrival of one of my most important visitors – Sam, the physiotherapist. A gently spoken Tamil, he had a cherubic face and an excellent command of English. Quite quickly, I had got some movement back in my right arm, but my leg was much more tender. For some reason, the doctors had decided against a traditional plaster cast and so I had to be very careful not to jolt the bone as it mended. Initially, I worked passively with a large electrical contraption that, for twenty minutes or so each morning, gently steered my leg back and forth. Later, Sam devised a programme of active stretches and bends to strengthen my muscles. Just as importantly, he helped keep my motivation up during the times when I began to drift and doubt my recovery.

For, despite the distraction of all these visitors and activities, I still had plenty of time on my hands. Yes, I had a television, books and a walkman, but I still got bored and frustrated sometimes and would lie staring miserably at the wall, getting irritable with the nurses, and wondering when I could get out of this place.

Grateful as I was for the support of the hospital staff and the presence of new friends, I still felt alone in a foreign world. And whilst the physical pain from the accident and operation was bearable, the psychological impact of what had happened to me continued to reverberate through the long, silent hours of the night. Often I woke sobbing in the dark, and felt my whole body throbbing as it began to release the shock and trauma of the battering it had taken.

While the physical discomfort was real enough, I began to see that I had some choice in how I responded to my suffering. And with that insight came a new spirit of appreciation and acceptance. Tired as I was from patchy sleep, I started to rejoice inwardly at the arrival of each new day. I also found myself trying to articulate my feelings of gratitude through spontaneous prayers and poems of thanks.

My state of confinement and dependence was providing an opportunity to examine myself and see what inner resources I really possessed. I had time to consider some of the big questions that stand silent behind the restless activity of our daily lives. What do I believe about how the world works? Why do "bad" things happen to us, and what can we learn from them? How much faith do I have in my fellow human beings? And how much faith in myself? Above all, I wondered how I could tap deeper into the power of healing that even now was working in and around me.

Lying in a hospital bed on the Indian subcontinent, I started to look at my life in a new way. The whining, angry cry "Why me?", which had become something of a mantra throughout my thirties, now found its counterpoint in a softer voice which hinted at a larger scheme in which my misfortunes were just brief, unhappy episodes. I started to appreciate too how the failures and difficulties in my past had, in fact, often nudged me back onto a more authentic path.

Now, as I reviewed the reversals of my trip, as well as the apparently chance meetings and coincidences, I wondered if I was being led towards some grand resolution. "A surprising victory." Wasn't that what the fortune-teller had predicted? I couldn't get the image of the Matrimandir at Auroville out of my head. This was, after all, where I felt I was being led. What better place for a scene of self-realization? And I had already got so close!

I had to be careful that all this introspection didn't lead to self-indulgent ego-tripping. Other human beings were implicated in my story: there had, for example, been two people involved in this road accident. I asked Vasu one day if he knew what happened to the driver of the motorbike that hit me. Apparently the other guy, a youth barely out of his teens, had hurt his wrist, though not badly. But his bike had fared less well.

Thinking back to the moments leading up to the collision, I knew my U-turn in the road had not been too clever. Still, that left the question of how the other rider had managed to hit me. Vasu had hinted that the biker might have been driving on the wrong side of the road. So who was responsible? And did it really matter?

At no point in the aftermath of the accident had the police been involved, and I got nowhere in my telephone calls to my insurance company in England who refused my claim on the basis that riding a scooter was classified as a "dangerous sport". The youth was not seeking any compensation (and I would certainly get nothing from him), so the matter was dropped. I had arranged for my scooter, which had also taken a battering, to be taken back to the hotel in Pondy, but I heard nothing from its owner there and so let that matter go too.

After a couple of weeks, I'd adapted to the rhythm of hospital life and made progress to the point where I could manoeuvre myself out of bed and use a zimmer frame to hop forward tentatively. Each day brought a small, but significant achievement. I remember hobbling over to the window one morning to get my first view of the outside world in a fortnight. I peered out of my third-floor window and was stunned by the brightness and clarity of the scene. I had to screw up my eyes against the dazzling canvas of a deep blue sky, on which were painted tall trees and shining buildings. In the middle distance, cream-coloured Ambassadors trundled past, while little figures bustled purposefully across the foreground. I felt inspired to start sketching and painting again, trying to capture some of the magic and newness of what I saw.

Another milestone was making it to the toilet on my own. Of all the limitations my injuries had placed on me, the enforced use of a bedpan had probably been the most challenging. I insisted on using it unaided, and therefore had to contort myself with only two working limbs into a position where it was actually possible to go.

I was now out of bed for some time each day, shuffling round in my zimmer frame. I also had a wheelchair and relished zipping around the hospital in it. No one seemed to mind me hogging the lift or rolling along the corridors between the various wards and departments. On my first trip outside the building, I nearly cried with the joy of feeling warm sun and cool breeze on my skin again! Nevertheless, I was daunted at the thought of having, at some point, to leave the safety of this controlled environment and the availability of round-the-clock help. The challenge of life beyond the hospital seemed immense; I didn't know where I would stay, let alone how I would clothe, feed and look after myself.

The next step was getting onto crutches, but my arms and shoulders burned with pain under the effort of hoiking myself around on them. The doctors reassured me that I was doing well, and the ward manager suggested I think of moving on shortly. I knew too that psychologically it would be healthy to break from a routine which had become somewhat institutionalized. The hardest decisions I had to make each day were which television channel to watch, and what type of curry to order for lunch. Still, here at PIMS at least, I felt special; out there I'd be just another tourist, and a disabled one at that.

I knew that worrying about these things would not help me, and reminded myself I was not alone. Friends were asking around and had already come up with one or two leads for places to stay. Sam had told me about a Catholic college nearby which had spare rooms and some staff support, but it didn't appeal to me greatly. Irmgard meanwhile had been checking out rooms in Auroville, and one day mentioned a place called "Centre Guest House" (CGH). She described it to me as clean and friendly, set in woodland near the centre of the community, and close to important sites like the Matrimandir and Visitor Centre. It sounded ideal.

I rang the Guest House manager, Saravanam, and began to introduce myself. 'Oh, Mr Jon,' he interrupted, 'I am so pleased to hear from you. I know all about your situation.' He went on to tell me he had a room available the following week. Three meals would be provided daily, with laundry and cleaning taken care of. The price, while not cheap, seemed reasonable for the comfort and security offered. I asked him to hold the room for me.

'Of course, Mr Jon, it would be my honour. You are our most

esteemed guest.'

As the date for discharge rushed towards me, I grew terrified at the prospect of having to leave the safe womb of the hospital for the bright glare and noise of the outside world. There could be no turning back now: I simply had to trust in what was coming. Auroville was at last opening its doors to me. I might have to limp in, bandaged and bruised, but I too could now enter the City of the Future.

Centre Guest House

The morning came when I packed up my things, settled my bill and said goodbye to the people I'd got to know around the hospital. I could now move around independently, either on crutches or with my zimmer frame, and I felt triumphant as I walked out of the building on my own. I climbed into Vasu's rickshaw and, as we set off, met his eyes in the rear-view mirror. I think he was nearly as excited as I was, perhaps even a little proud too to be the one co-ordinating my move. We pulled out of the hospital campus, sped along the country lane, and joined the main East Coast Road heading back towards Pondicherry.

Here was India again – colourful, chaotic, and noisy. As we drove, I took in the villages and shops, the land and trees, the people and animals; but everything now seemed even more vivid than I remembered. And that included the smell! The breeze coming off the ocean was mingled with exhaust fumes and the unmistakable whiff of less-than-fresh seafood. Along the roadside, vendors were laying out their fish on stones under the hot sun, with only umbrellas and cold water to keep the produce cool.

I caught a glimpse of a young mother in a doorway, swaying as she held an infant at her hip. Outside a café sat an old man with his legs crossed, sipping chai as he read the newspaper. Laughing children chased a dog along the roadside, their thin brown limbs cutting the air as they moved. I took it all in hungrily – looking with a little more gratitude and appreciation on the life unfolding all around me. Then my reverie was shattered by a torrent of hooting.

'For God's sake Vasu, slow down!' I shouted, as our rickshaw swerved over the road.

'No problem, Jon. You want, I slow down.' He eased his foot a little on the gas, but I was on edge as vehicles continued to weave around us – though always, it seemed, managing to pull into free space and keep the flow moving. I felt sadness and anger too as I saw the vulnerability of others on the road, particularly the women and children crammed precariously on the back of motorcycles. Not one of them was wearing a crash helmet.

Soon, we turned off the main road and entered Auroville. The rickshaw bumped along dry mud tracks and sent up clouds of reddish dust behind us. We crossed patches of scorched, arid scrub into the shade of woodland, passing little settlements as we went. I saw a shopping street with stalls displaying fruit, clothes and crafts; then a taxi rank, cash-point and several cafés, full of chilled-out young Westerners. Beyond the village stood a lake, adorned with bright pink lotuses, where Indians bathed under the mournful gaze of water buffalo resting on the bank.

As we drove, I saw signs in a mixture of English, French and Tamil advertising projects and facilities with names like Aurolec (the Auroville Electric company), La Piscine, and Pour Nous – the co-operative supermarket. Individual communities bore such names as Aspiration and New Creation, and I felt the same promise of a fresh start in Auroville that had attracted pioneers decades before, and which continued to draw people from all over the world.

We came to a stop in the car park of Centre Guest House, where we were greeted by a smiling, smartly dressed Indian holding an infant in his arms. Behind him, as if lined up for inspection, stood a group of men and women – the staff, I assumed. The man stepped forward, his hands pressed together as if in prayer. 'Namaste, Mr Jon!' I felt honoured to be greeted with this word of devotion and respect. 'I am Saravanam and this is my daughter, Kalyani. Welcome to our guest house. As you can see, we are all delighted that you are staying with us.' He extended his arm to take in the workers, who also saluted me. 'Come now, Mr Jon, I will show you to your room.'

Saravanam waved away the little crowd as Vasu helped me out of the rickshaw. I stood with my zimmer frame, surveying the cool green space in which CGH stood. A twisting concrete path led from the car park towards a complex of buildings nestling in young forest. Saravanam led the way while I shuffled along behind him. Then came Vasu with my rucksack and crutches. As we went, Saravanam pointed out the facilities at CGH.

I was impressed with what I saw. But in my new-found freedom, I stopped looking where I was going. The path suddenly dipped, the zimmer frame wobbled, and I felt myself going over. I thrust out my leg – my injured leg – to steady myself, then cried out as a stabbing pain shot through me. Vasu shouted out in alarm while Saravanam turned and lurched towards me, extending his arm for support. I regained my balance and felt my knee smarting. Had I just undone several weeks' worth of healing? Gradually the pain subsided and I could hobble forward once again. But now I kept my eyes firmly on the ground.

We arrived at my room, which was at the end of a neat row of apartments. The interior was airy and spacious. There were two low beds, a table and chairs, and a desk with a lamp and a telephone. I had a simple en suite bathroom and a veranda overlooking a patio shaded by tall trees. I told Saravanam I would be delighted to stay.

Vasu and I spent a couple of hours setting things up and unpacking. When he left, I sat down on the edge of the bed and sighed. At last, I'd made it to Auroville! I was excited to be on my own again. There'd be no nurses and doctors bustling around day and night; here I would be left alone to complete my recovery and explore Auroville as best I could.

But tripping on the path outside had shaken my confidence. I also felt a bit annoyed. Why weren't the paths here level? The incident was a wake-up call; a warning at the beginning of my convalescence in the community to take extra special care of myself. I had yet to realise that most of the outside world is not designed for the disabled.

During my first few days at CGH, I hardly ventured out. A friendly Tamil cook, named Dass, brought my meals to my room, and Saravanam came every day to enquire after my health. I practised walking around the room with my zimmer frame or on crutches. I sat out on the veranda, enjoying the simple woodland setting. The dominant colours were the clear, bright cobalt of the sky, and the dazzling gold of the Eastern sun, already strong by mid-morning. Then came a canopy of dusty green leaves and, closer to the ground, a variety of shrubs and large-petalled flowers.

After the institutional hush of the hospital, I also had to get used to a new soundscape – particularly at night and early in the morning. There was the insistent and alarming shriek of the "fever-bird" (so called because it drove the English colonials mad as they lay in fever with their tropical diseases), which would build in pitch and intensity only to stop suddenly, then resume a few moments later. Another type of bird specialised in percussive effects and I often heard a pair of them calling to one another – creating a pulse of sound moving in and out of phase with itself. Frogs, geckos, cats and dogs, mosquitoes, butterflies, spiders, cicadas and even the odd snake made their home here too.

As I grew more confident moving about, I ventured outside and began to explore the buildings and grounds around CGH. I visited the canteen where I joined the other guests for meals three times a day. It was good to have company again – particularly that of other European travellers who themselves had been drawn to Auroville.

Sometimes I went into the office to use the computer, and would spend a little time chatting with Saravanam, who was keen to improve his English. Most of all I enjoyed sitting in the central grove where a patio had been furnished with a chair and benches. Tall trees provided welcome shade, with a huge old banyan making a striking centrepiece. Dotted around the circle were small statues and shrines adorned with fresh flowers.

Vasu came regularly to take me out in the rickshaw. As we drove around, I began to get an idea how Auroville was laid out and being developed. I learned the whereabouts of the community's main public buildings such as the Town Hall and Post Office. I also discovered that many of the places I wanted to visit had no disabled access.

One day, I arrived at the main library to find a set of steps descending steeply into the building. It might have been just possible to get down them with crutches, but trying with a zimmer frame would have been suicidal. I called out for the librarian. A tall Westerner appeared at the bottom of the stairs.

'Ya? Zer is a problem here?' The man's German accent perhaps made him sound more impatient than he really was.

'Well, yes, actually. I'd like to use the library but I can't get in!'

He apologised and could offer no solution, and I left feeling frustrated. How could a community which prides itself as existing for all humanity be so limited in the facilities it offered those who have special needs?

Meanwhile, I had become aware of the many events and workshops going on around Auroville – most of which I also couldn't access. Righteous anger started to bubble away in me, and with it some resentment at my fate. Here I was at last, in the City of the Future, only to find myself a second-class citizen. The faith and optimism I'd cultivated during my stay in hospital were being nibbled at by cynicism. And sometimes, as I sat reading through the long evenings, I began to hear the soft scratching of depression at my door.

Saravanam told me that an senior Aurovilian, named Susmita, wanted to meet me. The following afternoon I greeted a mature but sprightly Italian woman, smiling and waving as she climbed off a vespa. We sat under the banyan tree and drank tea. In her sing-songy English, Susmita told me how she had survived polio as a child. Later she became interested in eastern spirituality and lived for some time at the Pondicherry Ashram before moving to Auroville. Though essentially able-bodied herself (she was very proud to be able to drive about on her "scooty" as she called it), she was determined to make Auroville a more accessible place. To this end she had established a working group – the "New Abilities Link", and was now looking for support. She asked me if I'd help her write press releases and other documents. She also wanted to use me as a case study and later arranged for photos to be taken of me strategically stranded at the bottom of the stairs in various buildings!

I told Susmita about my journey, and how I had felt drawn to the Matrimandir. I recounted my thrill at first seeing the temple and my disappointment over not being allowed in. Now I was resident in Auroville, I was entitled to enter. 'But as you know,' I grumbled, 'it isn't always easy to get into places round here!'

'Don't worry about that, Jon. We'll get you inside. You have been called here – it is the Mother's will.'

Maybe it was, I'm not sure, but I was certainly prepared to accept Susmita's help. For there was just one little problem: the designers of the most spiritually advanced structure in the universe had not thought to install a wheelchair ramp to get into it. Susmita told me not to worry; she had friends working at the temple who would see to it that I was not refused entry on account of my disability. An appointment was arranged for the following week. At last I was being granted permission to penetrate the very heart of the Auroville dream. What, I wondered, would I find there?

Into the Heart

I had showered, trimmed my hair and beard, and dressed in my best clean white clothes: today, I was going into the Matrimandir! Vasu arrived early, smiling broadly, and had also taken care with his appearance – wearing a freshly pressed driver's uniform in khaki. We were silent with excitement as we drove the short distance to the entrance of the gardens in which the Matrimandir sits like an enormous cosmic beacon. There was already a straggly queue of visitors extending down the road.

Vasu pulled over and I clambered out of the rickshaw, my crutches clattering around me. I looked up to see a pair of uniformed guards running towards us.

'No, no!' shouted one of the men, 'you are waiting here, Mr Jon. We are bringing you a chairwheel.'

A chairwheel? I thought, and then remembered Susmita's comment that I would be escorted in a special wheelchair that was kept in the office at the entrance to the temple. Whilst Vasu was off parking his rickshaw, the guards returned with a contraption that looked as if it had last seen service in the First World War. I dropped onto the sagging canvas of the seat and tried to smile as I was trundled, bumping and squeaking, along the stony path. I might as well have been wheeled in on a tea trolley for all the dignity it afforded. Still, I was being promoted to the front of the queue.

I was set down amongst a group of young Indian women –

students, I guessed – decked out in pristine shalwar kameez and adorned with flowers. After some moments of shyness, pointing and giggling, one of them stepped towards me.

'Good morning, sir. May I ask, you are coming with us into the Matrimandir?'

'I hope so. If I can get in!' I shrugged, smiled and patted the arm of the wheelchair.

'Oh, we are hoping so too, sir.' With a simple gesture the girl took off her ley (garland) and hung it around my neck. I felt honoured.

By now Vasu had caught us up. He grinned when he saw me and then commandeered the wheelchair, ready for the next part of our journey. A few minutes later a guide arrived and ushered the first twenty of us in the queue into the manicured gardens. He began to describe the design and construction of the Matrimandir. "The building you see before you... the gold on the roof... the world's greatest..." But it was impossible not to be distracted by the presence of the enormous, shimmering orb itself – glowing nearby in the morning sun and seeming to radiate a silent, pulsing energy that grew in intensity as we drew closer. The guide droned on, but I was already gone. This was my time to connect with the Source, to forge a link with the Spirit of the Universe. My whole life had been but a preparation for this moment!

Ahead of us, a paved path led straight down into a doorway at the base of the globe. Here, Vasu and a temple assistant lifted me bodily out of the wheelchair and, supporting me on either side, carried me over the threshold. Just inside the entrance, four handsome Tamil youths were waiting with a kind of sedan chair. These were my carriage bearers, appointed to carry me up to the inner chamber of the Matrimandir. On closer inspection I could see that my carriage was, in reality, an old bath chair suspended on two poles with a dirty white sheet thrown over it. But who was complaining? Right now I was the maharaja being borne aloft on his throne, high above the common herd and their petty concerns. Onwards and upwards, I thought, Destiny beckons!

Unfortunately, the youths were also getting a little carried away with themselves. As we ascended the long winding ramp into the heart of the edifice, they fell out of step and my sedan began to swing precariously from side to side. I clung onto the arms of the chair, and had only to turn my head slightly to look down over the rails of the ramp into the void. I gulped at the dizzying drop through space to the concrete floor far below. Oblivious to my terror, Vasu and several temple officials marched merrily behind us, followed by the pretty young students and the rest of the tour party all shuffling along in their socks.

At the end of a long climb, we finally reached the entrance to the "inner chamber" where our unlikely procession halted. I was set down on one side of a thickly carpeted lobby, equal parts science fiction and posh hotel. Everything was cool and white, and bathed in air-conditioned silence. With smiles and bows, the rest of the party filed slowly past me to go inside.

I could feel my heart thumping as I was transferred into a simple wooden chair. Any moment now, I too would enter into the inner sanctum! The thick heavy doors to the meditation chamber were drawn open and my chair was carried forwards into a muted darkness.

As my eyes adjusted to the gloom, I saw we were in a large circular hall, dimly lit and hermetically hushed. Around the room, a ring of huge marble columns rose high into the air. A creamy carpet provided a soft floor where my entourage had already arranged themselves in meditation posture.

As if all this were not sufficiently otherworldly, at the very centre of the room stood a metre-high crystal ball supported on a golden stand. The structure had been positioned directly under an aperture in the domed roof, thirty feet above. A single shaft of sunlight poured down on the sphere – creating a magical glow. For some minutes I sat, mesmerised by the spectacle. Then I remembered I had come here to meditate. I closed my eyes and went inside myself.

As I became aware of the weight of my body and steadied my breathing, a succession of images began to rise in my mind's eye. At first, there were little more than dull swirls of colour; abstract forms arranging themselves into elusive patterns that then dissolved. My limbs were growing heavier, my breathing deeper.

Then, like photographs being developed in the chemical bath of a darkroom, faces seemed to appear from the medley of shapes. Here was Aslam with his winning grin; there, Doctor Mini – chubby and beatific; Ram Dass made an appearance, alongside other characters I had met along my journey. Sometimes a scene would start to play itself out until I recalled myself to the meditation. I found myself thinking about lunch and briefly opened my eyes. The entire chamber was poised in silent stillness. In the twilight around me sat a multitude of figures – absorbed in their own being. The crystal ball shimmered gently. I breathed and brought myself back within.

Limb by limb, I felt my way mentally around my body. When I reached my left leg, there was a heavy throbbing, pulling my attention into it. In-between my breaths, snatches of remembered music revolved in irritating loops, whilst random words and phrases scrolled past like karaoke lyrics. Then more faces: this time, the sympathetic and long unseen eyes of families and friends back home. On went the breath: in, out… in, out…

Gradually, beneath this inner kaleidoscope of perceptions, something deeper, more visceral, began to call my attention. It began as a vague feeling of unease, deep in my stomach, and seemed to rise slowly and rhythmically into my chest. I breathed with it, synchronising myself with its motion. Dark and velvety, the impulse gained momentum. A growing sense of – what was it? Grief? was threatening to engulf me. At the same time, I was aware of a pain in my heart – a pulling at long-held tightness. I just about managed to come back to the breath.

The surging from the depths continued. I watched one wave – dark and heavy – rise and recede. I allowed it to come and go; felt it growing, half-welcomed it. Now I was riding on its crest, elated, even as its turbulent waters were filling my chest. I struggled to keep breathing. Recalling an instruction I'd once read in a yoga book, I tried to focus on a point in the middle of my forehead – the so-called "third eye".

Still the wave grew, oily black and swelling massively until it seemed to tower over me. It moved with a roaring sound, swallowing everything in its wake until it seemed to contain, in its great elemental mass, everything I most feared and desired in the Universe. My heart felt about to burst. An almighty "Yes!" and an equally powerful "No!" struggled for expression from the core of my being. I couldn't hold the wave back any longer and surrendered as the next great surge burst the banks of my heart. I heard a strangled sob tear itself from my throat, my mind plunged into blackness and my body went limp.

I was alone in a silent void where all sense of time and space had dissolved. Then I began to be aware of pinpoints of light that grew slowly and seemed to be dancing around me. As I watched, the fragments began to crystallize into a matrix of harlequin diamonds, spinning slowly in the air. It was like being in a circus "hall of mirrors", but instead of distorted reflections of my face and body, I was looking at different aspects of my personality. Here was the kind Jon, there the anxious Jon; here the happy soul, there the sad, lonely man. On display too, were all the roles I'd played in my life: the son, the brother, the teacher, the friend...

I became mesmerized by the dancing diamonds and realised that I was seeing my own sense of self – fragile, shifting and temporary. As I watched, I wondered what was holding this kaleidoscope of shapes together. I was gripped with a sudden terror. *What was to stop these pieces winking out of existence altogether?* Slowly, the fear gave way to curiosity. If this shimmering mirage really was me, then Who, or What, was actually looking at it?

Before I had time to solve this riddle, my eyes opened and I found myself back in the Matrimandir. I could see Vasu standing over me, could feel his hand gently rocking my shoulder, and hear his voice whispering my name. Behind him hovered two or three temple assistants, looking on with concern. Some of the meditators had turned to look at me, whilst others continued serenely in their practice. The crystal ball continued to glow gently, unchanging in its luminous alchemy. I could feel tears on my cheeks, but I knew too that I was smiling.

At the same time as feeling emotion, I seemed also to be watching this little drama with a detached, though kindly, irony. I was aware that an overwrought, middle-aged Englishman – who just happened to be me – was having a "breakthrough" (or was it a breakdown?) experience in a futuristic meditation temple in a spiritual community in India. It was no big deal. These things happen every day. The commotion I was causing was both cosmic and commonplace.

I felt myself gently carried out of the chamber and placed in a more modern wheelchair. Then I was wheeled down the long ramp and carried outside into the glare of the sun. I rejoiced in the heat on my skin as Vasu pushed me on a slow ride through the gardens. Birds sang. Wisps of cloud hovered high overhead. I felt lighter and somehow expanded, as if my consciousness extended far beyond my physical body. We stopped to rest in a nearby grove, where ancient banyans provided a welcome shade. Minutes of silence passed.

'You alright now, Jon?' asked Vasu, his dark eyes filled with concern.

'Yes, Vasu. I'm fine.'

And I really was.

I spent the next few days in a pleasant state of openness and sensitivity quietly reflecting on my experience in the Matrimandir. I didn't want to talk much, or get involved in activities that would jar my delicate mood. It was a joy simply to wake in the morning and behold light coming in through the window. The splash of water on my face felt cooler and fresher than I had ever known. The flavours of food exploded in my mouth as I chewed.

I spent hours sitting alone on my veranda simply looking at nature. In their stillness and beauty, the trees and flowers seemed to express the possibility of peace and harmony; the birds, through their song and flight, told of ease and freedom. The earth showed me how to be firm and bear the weight of life, while the wide sky reflected my opened mind. Daily, the sun returned to remind me of the miracle of light, and by extension, the ever-present possibility of Illumination. Meanwhile, my own thoughts and feelings arose and passed away in a parade of insubstantial forms.

Slowly though, the everyday world began to impinge on my bliss. There were visitors to be entertained, physiotherapy sessions to organise, and writing work to be done with Susmita and the New Abilities Link. Meanwhile, friends and family in England wanted to know how, and what, I was doing. But how could I explain what I did not yet fully understand myself?

After toiling to reach the City of the Future, I had at last found my way to the heart of the dream. Now here I was, somewhat battered but strangely grateful for all I had experienced. And, in my own limited way, I was ready for action. The question was – what could I do here? And who would I be?

In the Community

I wanted to find out more about Auroville and its founders. After all, this is where I seemed to have been called; perhaps here I would be able to make sense of the shattering experiences of my journey.

I already knew a little about Sri Aurobindo and the Mother – the spiritual "parents" of Auroville. Both were fascinating characters. Aurobindo had received a late nineteenth-century education in England and been a brilliant scholar. On his return to India in 1893, he got involved with the movement for Indian independence and became one of the leading figures inspiring the younger generation towards a national consciousness. Unlike Gandhi, Aurobindo did not rule out the use of violence in the fight for freedom and, though innocent himself, he was jailed in 1908 following a terrorist bombing against the British. In prison he practised yoga and meditation, and made a decision to retire from worldly life. On his release, he settled in Pondicherry (then under French administration), and an ashram began to evolve around him.

The Mother (Mirra Alfassa) was born in Paris in 1878 to Turkish/Egyptian parents. She was a sensitive child, later training as a painter and also playing the organ. A member of the artistic and spiritual communities in Paris around the turn of the twentieth century, she went on to study occultism and Eastern philosophy. In 1914 she travelled to India and met Aurobindo, who became her guru. Later, she settled permanently in the Pondicherry ashram, first as a disciple, but then occupying more and more of a central role until 1926, when she became the chief authority there. After Aurobindo's death in 1950, the Mother began to evolve the vision for a new kind of spiritual community, and developed a practical blueprint for a "City of the Future" – to be named Auroville, which began to take shape from 1968.

So much for the facts, but what about the people – the so-called "Aurovilians"? Who were they? Why had they come? And what were they doing here?

Bill was a gruff Yorkshireman in his mid-sixties who had lived in Auroville since the early seventies. He often came for his lunch at the CGH canteen and always sat alone, reading a book after he had eaten. Saravanam had told me he was one of the pioneer Aurovilians and something of a legendary figure around the place. One day I went over to his table and introduced myself. 'May I join you for a moment?' I asked.

Bill looked up from his book. His face was lean and tanned; his blue eyes, clear and penetrating. He hesitated, looked me over, taking in the crutches. 'Sure, why not?'

I sat down. There was a long pause during which I wondered how to begin the conversation. Bill broke the silence. 'So how did you injure yourself?'

I related my experience of crashing the scooter and being in hospital. 'You were lucky,' he said, 'a friend of mine died on the East Coast Road last year.'

'I'm sorry.'

'Well,' he sighed, 'we get used to it. There's some kind of accident there pretty much every week.'

I told him how, ironically, it had been the accident that had brought about my stay in Auroville. Then I asked him how he had come to be here.

Bill had been on the hippy trail, a seeker. He had done the round of ashrams and gurus before finding his way to Pondicherry – drawn initially by Sri Aurobindo's philosophy, and then attracted by the Mother's promise of a new kind of life. He had some agricultural experience and had got involved with a farming project in which Westerners worked side-by-side with the local Indians. 'It's nothing like it was then, you know,' he explained with a gesture that took in the hall in which we were sitting, 'we had nowt when we started here!'

I had already seen some pictures from Auroville's earliest days: grainy black-and-white photos showing lean young Westerners in a barren landscape, squatting around fires, posing by ramshackle huts, or tending little vegetable patches. Bill had arrived full of energy and idealism and worked on a massive reforestation programme that slowly brought foliage and shade back to the scorched plain. Engineers and architects followed, then teachers, artists and craftspeople. Local Indians found employment as labourers and farmhands.

Amidst the hope and optimism of a new life, Bill explained, there had been trouble too. The elite of Aurobindo's ashram in Pondicherry had never been altogether in favour of the Mother's brainchild developing up the road. And now they faced the problem of trying to maintain spiritual authority over a diverse and expanding international community.

Within Auroville itself, there were tensions around how to reconcile the Mother's original vision with the changing conditions and evolving culture of the new community. Bill was concerned about the ecological aspects of "growing a city" – in particular the limited freshwater supply which was in danger of being contaminated by seawater. Then there was the issue of increased traffic and roadbuilding, not to mention the vague, but threatening, murmurings about climate change and its effect on the monsoon.

Bill saw two distinct perspectives at work: the top-down approach of planners and administrators – many of whom could be seen behind their computers in the Town Hall, and the bottom-up approach of the community members and their grassroots projects. He wondered if these two visions could ever be harmonised.

I felt something of this tension myself on my visits to projects around Auroville. I spent a morning at "Buddha's Garden" – a small organic farm run by an energetic Englishwoman, Priya. As I worked alongside a small team of volunteers picking cashew fruits, I learned what a struggle it had been to get the project established. Initially, there had been little support from the central authorities, and the enterprise still faced challenges over the distribution and marketing of its products within Auroville.

At "Sadhana Forest", on the periphery of the community, the emphasis was on land reclamation and harvesting rainwater. At the helm was an Israeli family with strong pioneering instincts and an uncompromising ecological philosophy. On the evening I visited, there was a tour of the site followed by a film and shared meal. It was inspiring to meet people from all over the world drawn to this little slice of Utopia, but sobering to learn to what extent the project was running on a shoestring and dependent on the generosity of visitors and all-too-rare grants. As in so many idealistic endeavours, the danger of burnout seemed to hover over the minority of really dedicated members of the community.

Saravanam was an example of the type of educated Indian who had been attracted by the Auroville vision. He had been living and working at CGH for five years and had started a family there. As a trained accountant and administrator, he had clear ideas about how he wanted to see things develop and felt that in order to have more influence he would need to improve his English.

Sometimes he and I would get together after lunch to study some of the Mother's writings. Saravanam would read for a bit, I'd correct any obvious mistakes in his pronunciation, and then we'd discuss the passage. I found much of the Mother's advice helpful; for example, her emphasis on the individual's capacity to take charge of his or her own life through such techniques as mindfulness and meditation. Other of her views I found more difficult to accept or understand. She seemed to take a dim view of sexuality for example, and also pushed certain ideas around karma to dubious conclusions. Is it really acceptable to state that infants born with defects of one kind or another are merely manifesting the state of consciousness of the parents at the moment of conception?

I wondered what happened to children with special needs in Auroville and found they were not integrated into the mainstream schools. But there was an excellent facility for local Indian village children with disabilities. I got to spend a morning there and was impressed with the love and care with which the youngsters were being treated.

I also visited a primary school where Indian and Western Aurovilian children were taught together. The place was reminiscent of a Rudolf Steiner school, with its emphasis on educating the whole child and cultivating the imagination and senses. The atmosphere was informal and the children seemed confident and relaxed. The day began with meditation and chanting; later, in the warm outdoors, the children presented a play – on an environmental theme – which they'd written themselves. They seemed to possess a passionate and inspiring vision for a better world.

As I made my visits around Auroville, I began to form my own picture of a complex organism, evolving day by day. Even if it wasn't quite Paradise, it was still thoroughly progressive and aspirational.

Occasionally though, I heard stories of the struggles between different sections of the community. Some of these may have reflected the inescapable legacy of colonialism, and the material inequality between incoming Europeans and local Indians. Of course, not all the foreigners who had settled in Auroville were wealthy. In fact, many of them had abandoned more prosperous lives in the West to buy into the community under terms that would make returning to live in their native countries difficult. There were also many visitors from other countries living extremely simply and volunteering their time and energy for weeks or even months.

Nevertheless, it was impossible to ignore the fact that in the hierarchy of the settlement, it seemed to be Europeans – above all, French and Germans – who mostly occupied the senior positions, while Indians provided a lot of the labour. I often saw groups of village women – some quite elderly – squatting at the roadside, breaking stones for surfacing. I suspected they spent the whole day at the task and were paid little for their effort.

One day, Vasu drove me to an area where large, modern-looking villas sat in expansive, manicured grounds. 'This where the bosses living!' he told me. Yet, not five minutes down the road stood dirt-poor villages where life had not changed much in centuries. It was not surprising to hear that there was a small, but growing problem of crime in Auroville.

I also wondered about the emphasis on spiritual purity and traditional morality. Might not such an idealistic society trip itself up by promoting human perfection above diversity and self-expression? Yes, Auroville was a "rainbow nation", and in many ways both experimental and alternative, but how tolerant would it be of other kinds of difference? Had any LGBT (lesbian, gay bisexual and transgender) folk made their home here?

Throughout my travels in India, I had struggled to know what was appropriate to say and ask about sexuality; there seemed an essential modesty and conservatism about the people I met – many of whom were practising Hindus and very family-minded. I had squirmed many times in the face of questions about my marital status, yet knew from reading newspapers that changes were afoot in Indian society. I had seen several articles on contraception, forced marriage and gay rights, as well as more lurid accounts of transsexualism and prostitution.

So it was a relief when Irmgard asked me one day if I was gay. She told me she had a gay son herself and that it was no big deal. She also said that groups of "beautiful boys" could be seen walking late at night down by the beach in Pondicherry. As far as she knew though, there was no visible gay presence in Auroville itself.

Should this have bothered me? Well, we were in the City of the Future after all – a place supposedly designed for all of humanity. But my concern went beyond the issue of personal freedom and sexual diversity. As in other developing countries, the issue of HIV is extremely serious in India, and the situation is not helped by secrecy and shame. In all of the reading I'd done about Auroville, I'd seen no references to sex or sex education, other than a piece in an educational anthology for children which imagined a humanity so far evolved that sex would be redundant, and procreation an entirely spiritual affair!

My physical recovery was going well. The transition from zimmer frame to two crutches, and then to one crutch, meant I could now move faster, go up and down stairs and generally participate a bit more in things. And the more I got out and met people, the more I sensed new possibilities for myself. I had heard that English teachers were always needed in Auroville, and there could be some musical opportunities too. I began to wonder if I might actually stay here.

It was now mid-April and I had been in India nearly four months. I worked out that I could probably afford to live at CGH until July. But the monsoon was not far off, and would bring with it a stifling heat that forced people indoors for several hours in the middle of each day. Some activities at Auroville were already winding down a bit. How would it feel to live here in the quieter months when there was little to do but sit and watch the rain?

Yet the thought of starting a new life here was seductive. How many of us have not fantasized at one time or another about stepping out of our lives and beginning again? Or simply staying somewhere we've visited on holiday, or while travelling, and seeing how life unfolds from there…

Along with these thoughts, a powerful sense of confusion began to hit me. Where was I trying to get to anyway? I remembered my original intention to visit the holy Buddhist sites of northern India. Should I try to see them before leaving the country? Or should I go straight to my sister in Australia where I knew I would be better looked after? Should I even be thinking of flying in my condition? Beneath these questions were more basic ones: why had I come to India in the first place? And had I found what I was looking for? What I really needed was someone to help me make sense of all I had experienced. Only, who?

Last days

One day, Irmgard told me she had a friend I should meet. 'He is a very nice man, I think you will like him,' she said with a smile.

The following day we all met at one of the cafés not far from CGH. Opposite me sat Lars, a tall Dane about my own age. His height and blonde good looks gave him an almost exotic appearance amongst the tanned Westerners and Indians that sat around us. During the conversation he told me he was a corporate trainer whose work took him all over the world. 'I come to Auroville to escape from it all,' he laughed, 'only, people here keep asking me to sort out their lives for them!'

I told him about my trip and was pleased to notice how attentive he was, nodding sympathetically and chuckling from time to time at my account. 'Wow,' he said as I wound up the story, 'that's some journey!' He smiled at me and I saw in his eyes some flicker of kindly recognition. I asked him, half-jokingly, if he would help me sort out my life. He said he'd be happy to try and suggested we meet the following week.

It was late afternoon. We sat on the roof terrace of La Cantine, sipping tea and looking out over Auroville. The sun was low and cast a mellow glow over the trees.

I had been surprised to find myself dressing up a little for the occasion, and now felt slightly nervous in front of this handsome Viking. Lars fixed me with his powerful gaze. 'So, Jon, tell me one thing you've learned from your trip, one thing you'd like to do with your life, and one thing that frightens you.'

I thought for a minute or two. Then the answers tumbled out. 'I've learned that I can trust people more than I think. I'd like to write a book about what I've experienced in India. I'm frightened to leave Auroville.'

Lars laughed. 'Good answers! I don't really think you need someone to sort out your life for you, but we could work on the bit about leaving here.'

We spent the next hour working through some of my anxieties about what lay beyond Auroville. It was only natural to feel confused about the change coming. I'd heard stories of some of the difficulties encountered by other European travellers on their return home from the East. A German friend had mentioned the depression that overcame her when she saw the dull, straight lines and clean streets of her hometown in Bavaria. Most of all though, it was the people and atmosphere that jarred. 'They just don't know how lucky they are,' she had claimed, 'driving around in their Mercedes with their miserable faces, complaining about the weather...'

Here, in the magic bubble of Auroville, it was easy to hold up the idealism of the community against the cynicism of the world beyond. From the colourful vantage point of Eastern spirituality, Western life could appear pale and grey. It was the old argument about faith versus reason.

Yet there was a danger of over-romanticising and over-simplifying, for in one sense Auroville itself reflected both the Western emphasis on progress through material improvement, and the Eastern bias towards self-realisation through spiritual means. The Matrimandir was a symbol of this: a colossally expensive, ultra-modern building dedicated to meditation.

I knew Auroville was hardly representative of India as a whole, and that after my long convalescence – first in hospital, and then in the community – I would soon have to face once again the reality of the country outside of its institutions.

From time to time Vasu would take me on a trip into Pondicherry, but on these occasions he wanted me to see the Indian, not the French, city. A muddy canal was all that separated the "black" district, full of teeming humanity, noise and colour, from the wide, tree-lined boulevards of the former colony.

On one occasion we visited the botanical gardens, but they were nothing like those I'd seen back in Ooty. Instead of the healthy trees and carefully tended lawns of the ex-British hill station, here I saw only bare, dusty earth punctuated with a bit of sad vegetation. There was litter everywhere and several dodgy-looking characters milling about aimlessly.

Right outside the gardens was a disused market where some beggars had found a refuge, sleeping in the squalid booths lining the pavements. Yet just across the road were signs of the "new" India – air-conditioned coffee shops and shiny, modern office blocks. There was an intensity about the juxtaposition of rich and poor that was hard to bear. Vehicles sped past oblivious. Everything seemed so bright, fast and noisy. Though I was fascinated by what I saw, I knew I could not stay here much longer. But, however uncomfortable it was to be in India, I was still apprehensive about moving on to another continent, and a country I knew almost nothing about.

After a number of phone calls and visits to travel agents, I had managed to secure a flight to Melbourne leaving the following week from Delhi. To get there, I would need to take an internal flight from Chennai, about three hours away from Pondicherry. I made arrangements and began to focus on my departure.

Knowing I was leaving soon seemed to sharpen my perceptions. Every person I met and every place I went seemed charged with more meaning than I could grasp. And whilst I wanted to absorb as much as possible of the life unfolding around me in the time remaining, I knew also I must embark on a process of separation from the country and people that had been my whole world during these last months.

Vasu and I had known one another for a couple of months by now and had grown close. Of course, there was an economic aspect to our relationship too. I had become almost like an employer – using Vasu as a chauffeur and general assistant. Whilst Vasu never overcharged me, he understandably sought to earn as much as possible during my stay at Auroville; we were approaching the hot season and the number of visitors he could drive about would decline. I had to strike a balance between the generosity I felt (stemming from my gratitude for his rescuing me), and a cooler, more hard-headed approach which sought to discourage dependency.

It seemed that each visit from Vasu brought news of a further expense that needed meeting – whether it was the leaking roof on his house, or work that needed doing on the rickshaw. Then there were his children's clothes, the mobile phone his wife wanted… I knew that Irmgard had helped him out on occasions, but she had warned me the money wasn't always spent in the way it should have been.

So, when Vasu invited me to eat with him and his family at their house in the nearby village of Bomayapalayam, I hesitated initially. I wasn't sure I wanted our relationship to extend into his private life. But I realised I was being honoured with a unique opportunity, and accepted.

The following morning, Vasu came to pick me up with his two young sons. We all got in the rickshaw and went to collect fish from the market. The boys sat with me in the back, eyeing me nervously and giggling between themselves. Soon we swung off the main road and trundled down a narrow side street where locals sat outside their tumbledown houses, chatting and watching children playing in the street.

Vasu brought the rickshaw to a stop beside a thatched mud-hut set in a small compound overhung by gnarled, leafy trees. Near the entrance, on a raised platform in the shade, slept an old man.

'This my father,' said Vasu, pointing to the curled up figure. 'He bad leg too.' Apparently, he had been involved in a road accident many years previously but had not been able to afford proper treatment. 'He not walk properly now,' added Vasu.

I followed Vasu into the cool, dark interior of the small hut and looked around me. The first thing I noticed was a large television standing on a table to one side of the room. But there was no other furniture, just some woven mats that had been laid on the earth floor. One of the boys brought in a plastic chair for me to sit on.

After a couple of minutes, Vasu's wife came in from the back carrying cooking utensils. She greeted me shyly and began to prepare the fish and vegetables on a stove on the floor in front of us. Vasu went outside, returning with a great pot pluming steam and the smell of freshly cooked rice. We sat quietly until Vasu's young daughter came in, singing and laughing. She was a pretty little thing, less shy than her elder brothers, and came over to me with something in her hand. As she opened her balled fist, I saw the black and orange insect lying on her palm.

'Centipede!' I said.

'Pentypeed,' she echoed, and we laughed.

When the food was ready, Vasu brought in his father – a wizened, stooped figure who smiled at me and mumbled a few words in Tamil. I got to my feet and offered him the chair, but Vasu waved me to sit down again. I felt embarrassed as the whole family, including the old man, took their places sitting in a circle on the floor. The food was dished out and Vasu found a fork for me, as I still hadn't got used to eating with my fingers. Though I still felt a little awkward in the situation, I ate slowly – wanting to savour the food, and the experience.

After eating, Vasu showed me the adjoining room. There

wasn't much in there – just some folded clothes, bedding and bric-a-brac. I realised with a shock that this was, probably, the total sum of the family's possessions, and that within these two rooms unfolded the whole of their domestic life. Six people ate, slept, prayed and played in a space little larger than the typical front room of a British semi. As Vasu drove me back to CGH, I vowed never to forget what I had just seen.

The episode also inspired me to find more wholesome ways to help Vasu before I left India. I bought him a new pair of glasses, as well as taking him to the dentist to get his teeth fixed. Hopefully, stylish spectacles and a beaming smile would help him attract other customers in the future!

Whilst Vasu and his family had little choice in how they lived, others around Auroville were exploring simplicity as a spiritual practice. Asceticism remains a potent force in India, and during my travels I had heard extraordinary stories of people living on air or eating only potatoes, sleeping standing up or not talking for decades.

Just a few days before leaving the community, I found myself sitting in a café with a Buddhist nun from Korea who claimed not to have eaten for twelve years. There was nothing boastful about her manner and she looked to be in good health. Apparently, she'd simply experimented with her diet to the point where she found she could live on liquids alone. 'Oh, and I spend a lot of time in the Matrimandir...' she smiled, as if that fact explained the mystery.

She told me that much of what we think is necessary for our survival is actually conditioned by our upbringing and culture. This is obviously true for the material objects we surround ourselves with – cars and mobile phones, for example – but could it really apply to food as well? One part of me was sceptical – dismissing the woman as crazy; another side was intrigued by her story and wanted to investigate further. But time was running out and I felt there were more important things to do before leaving Auroville.

Though I had been back to the hospital for occasional check-ups, I now visited PIMS to say goodbye – proudly walking along the corridor and showing off my recovery to the doctors and nurses who had looked after me so well. Passing A&E, I recalled my own arrival there not so long ago, and felt keenly for the huddles of relatives and friends waiting outside for news of their loved ones.

Later that day, I gave an interview to Auroville Radio in which I talked about my experience in the community. I said my stay had been inspiring and that Auroville, with its abundance of visionary projects, fully deserved the epithet "City of the Future". Everything (apart from the issue of disabled access) was well organised, and the people here seemed to be genuinely happy and healthy.

I wondered too if there might be a place for a little anarchy or craziness from time to time. I hadn't seen or heard of anything resembling the kind of safety valve provided by events like Mardi Gras, Carnival or the Jewish Purim – festivals which sanction and structure extrovert (and occasionally outrageous) behaviour within the sometimes conformist confines of religion and community.

My own freedom was now being expressed through increased mobility. I could walk with just a stick for support and was even able to ride a bicycle. As I pedalled slowly along the sandy tracks linking one community project with another, I felt a joyful sense of returning strength and confidence. Yet, even as I was starting to feel normal again, I realized the long journey ahead of me would pose huge challenges. Taxis, airports and planes all seemed a bit daunting after my life as a convalescent.

As I prepared to become a traveller once again, I began to lighten my load. I had amassed a little collection of medical paraphernalia including crutches, weight cuffs, and even a TENS machine for pain relief; the local health clinic was happy to accept the lot. I also gave away clothes and books that I couldn't justify carrying to Australia.

The night before I was due to leave, I invited Lars to join me and my friends for supper at the CGH canteen. I felt not only gratitude for his support, but also a growing attraction which pleased and surprised me. The last thing I had expected to find at Auroville was romance! Susmita and Irmgard had said they would try to come too, in addition to several more people I had got to know around the community.

Six of us were already sitting at one of the long tables in the room when Lars' imposing figure appeared at the doorway. I called out to him. He waved and walked over to our table. He was wearing a matching Indian shirt and trousers in light blue cotton, with gold stitching around the neck and cuffs. He brought with him the scent of jasmine. I felt like a teenager on a first date.

After I made the necessary introductions, we all went to get our food from the serving hatch. Dass and the other cooks seemed to have excelled themselves tonight. In addition to the regular pots of rice, dhal, idli and sambar, there was a choice of salads, okra, curd and even some popadums and chutneys. The meal was great and the conversation flowed. I was happy.

After dinner we went to sit outside under the banyan tree. A nearly full moon hung overhead and cast a pale light over our circle. Our conversation was accompanied by the chirping of night insects. After an hour or so, my guests began to drift home, leaving their good wishes hovering in the warm darkness.

'You'll be careful with your leg, yes?'

'And come back to visit soon!'

'Please remember us when you are back in England...'

'Namaste, Jon.'

Lars had remained behind and the two of us sat in silence for a while. 'Isn't it strange,' he said, 'I go to Qatar next week, then back to Copenhagen. You'll be in Australia and then England…' His voice broke off. I was about to say something in reply, but as I turned towards him my arm slipped off the chair and our hands brushed one another. A tingle ran through me. We leaned towards one another and kissed.

My final morning in India had arrived. I had said goodbye to Lars, cleaned out my room and settled my account with Saravanam. I stowed my rucksack in the office; in a couple of hours time I would be back to collect it and meet the taxi which would take me to Chennai, sharing with an English couple who were also leaving CGH to fly home.

Now though, Vasu had come to take me to a nearby beach where chess players met at one of the shady cafés set back from the sea. Mr Perisswamy and his young son were already there, along with several other players I knew from previous visits. I sat down opposite Mr Kathir anticipating the usual thrashing he gave me every time we played.

'Ah, Mr Jon, I see you are coming back to learn another lesson!' he said, leaning back smugly in his chair. I drew white and played a standard opening, but within nine or ten moves my opponent had steered the game into unfamiliar territory. I sat, frowning at the board, confused by the possibilities.

At the next table was a group of children – two Indians and two Europeans, enjoying a game of their own. Though absorbed in the match, their faces were lit up with the pleasure of playing. I looked back at the board in front of me, softened my focus and smiled inwardly. The sound of the sea rolled on in the background.

Whereas I had always approached chess as a fierce mental contest for dominance, I now allowed myself to see the poetry of the game. Black and white may have been engaged in a battle, but there was no reason they shouldn't also dance from time to time. I breathed out slowly and felt my shoulders drop.

Under my relaxed gaze, each of my pieces seemed to take

on a more vibrant presence. My knights, for example, were not simply armoured horsemen thundering around the centre of the board, but graceful riders whose mounts jumped over a chequered arena. Behind them, my pawns had evolved from a company of dusty foot soldiers into a corps de ballet, linked in a chain, each supporting its neighbour. My king and queen lay safe in their castle, for the time being at least, oblivious to the threat to their kingdom. For a storm was massing on the horizon – a slow shadow, advancing down the stage and bringing with it a troupe of shadowy actors revelling in their power to disturb and distract.

Yet, as I continued to glance from white to black and back again, I could see the two forces as complementary, forming a whole. What had previously seemed rigid and polarised, now appeared fluid and dynamic. The board and pieces, the straight lines and angles of attack and defence, had transformed into an illuminated field of possibility – an energy flow mirroring the meeting of two minds.

I stopped trying to calculate only my own moves and focused instead on the totality of the situation. My intention was still to capture the enemy king, but this narrow objective had now widened to include all the pieces on the board. Of course, I had to be mindful that Mr Kathir, in contrast to my "soft" approach, was probably looking for the quickest way to smash through my defences and pulverize my king. But if I spent too much of my energy worrying about his intentions, I would never get clear about my own. Even here, on the chessboard, I was being asked to show some faith in myself, to step forwards into the unknown.

By now, the centre of the board had become a minefield which one wrong step could detonate. But I sensed that a bold move was necessary. Mr Kathir was, above all, a strategist; I would have to rely on something else. My white-square bishop seemed to be calling my attention and, not fully conscious of what I was doing, I stretched out my hand and advanced the piece deep into black territory. I sat back, breathed out a sigh, and waited for the fallout.

Mr Kathir paused, then looked up at me and frowned. What? I thought, but said nothing. Then, as I looked at the pieces, I too could see that the picture had now changed. That single move of the bishop had opened up a new channel from which all kinds of possibilities could flow. One of my rooks for example, which for the whole game had lain dormant on the back rank, was now looking out hungrily on an open file. And my queen, who until now had stayed faithfully by her king's side, could now consider stepping out on to the field – radiating majesty and power in all directions.

And so it went. The more I focused on doing the best I could with the resources I had available, the less I worried about winning or losing the game. When it was my turn, I calmly considered my options before allowing a more intuitive sense of "rightness" to guide my actions. When my opponent moved, I took time to absorb the change in the situation and the implications for me of the new position.

Mr Kathir, meanwhile, was growing visibly agitated. He shuffled in his seat, sipped sharply at his juice and tapped on the tabletop. His moves remained strong, but seemed to be made chiefly in response to the demands of my pieces. I realised, with a mixture of glee and alarm, that I was now calling the tune. All I had to do was hold my nerve.

Fifteen minutes later, with his defence in ruins, and defeat only a move or two away, my opponent was congratulating me on my uncharacteristically brilliant performance. 'You played different today, Mr Jon. Very good. Though I must say, I was not at my best.'

We laughed and shook hands. I recalled the words of Hamid the fortune-teller: "When all is said and done, you are making a surprising victory."

It was time to leave. I said goodbye to the other players and walked up the narrow lane from the sea towards the main road. I stood for a few minutes at the junction of the East Coast Road and the Auroville turning opposite. It was scorching hot, the sky ablaze, the road shimmering heat. I looked around me, fixing in my mind these final images of a scene I had come to know so well: the broad thoroughfare along which thundered every kind of vehicle; the stalls selling drinks and snacks; the ever-shifting crowd of Indians – standing, walking, sitting, talking. On the opposite pavement, a few drivers lay dozing in their rickshaws, their legs hanging lazily out the sides. A hundred yards further down the road was the fateful place where I had come off the scooter.

Life was going on as normal, but I would shortly be gone – just another visitor, like so many before and since. Yet I would take something of this with me, for in Auroville I had learned not only how to walk again, but perhaps also how to love. I felt an immense gratitude for my life, and for India. I had the feeling that one day I would return here – if not in this lifetime, then in another.

Epilogue

"India is a harsh mistress but she has no shortage of lovers."
Anon

Australia proved an enjoyable way to transition from Auroville back to life in the UK. I spent three happy weeks in Melbourne, staying with my sister and her family. What a contrast with India! The weather, for a start, was much cooler and I had to go clothes buying soon after I arrived. It wouldn't do to be seen strolling around St Kilda in a loincloth.

Everything in Oz looked modern and clean. The Melbourne city skyline resembled a film-set, its pristine architecture radiating youthful optimism. The cars seemed enormous, as did the houses, and the people looked well fed and satisfied.

One Saturday, I saw an advert in the paper for an "Emerging Writers' Conference", and rode into town to find out more. In the grand setting of Melbourne Town Hall, I mingled with aspiring authors, screenwriters and bloggers, and got excited listening to them talk about first novels, agents and publishers. I too had a story to tell and wondered if I might have a go at writing a book myself. Each evening, back at home after supper, I'd borrow my sister's computer and tap out a few paragraphs.

Three weeks later, I walked confidently off the plane at Heathrow, eager to pick up the threads of my former life. When I met with family and friends though, I found it hard to answer their questions.

'How did you get on, Jon?'

'Where was the best place you went?'

'Would you go back?'

I wanted to share my journey, but when I tried to describe my experiences, the result was flat and lifeless. The vibrancy of what I'd been through in India was fading as fast as my tan. I tried to keep my memories alive through writing, but as time passed it proved harder and harder to evoke the intensity of the sensations I'd felt on the other side of the world.

One day I went to pick up a parcel that I'd sent back from Kerala to a friend. I remembered having packed souvenirs and gifts – things I didn't want to cart around in my rucksack. I broke the seal on the package, unwrapped the cloth covering, then slit open the cardboard box within. A sweet breath of sandalwood wafted out. I closed my eyes and inhaled deeply. Apart from the incense inside, there was a carved soapstone Ganesha that I'd been given in Mysore, and a beautiful silk scarf I'd haggled for in the same city. Then some books: a guide to Hindu myths, manuals on Indian music and yoga. There were a few silk-paintings, some sketchbooks, and a handful of little gifts for my family – each item charged with the memory of places and people from my Indian odyssey.

I had kept a journal during my trip, done some sketches and taken lots of photos. Surely, with all this, I could reconstruct my journey in all its depth and colour? I kept writing, and the paragraphs grew into pages, the pages into chapters, and the chapters into a book. But though I could describe what had happened to me in India, I still hadn't discovered what it all meant!

I had gone to India with only the vaguest of notions of what to expect, yet I'd assumed that I would somehow be taken care of. Now, I began to see the challenges of my journey as a series of assaults on my sense of privilege, entitlement and independence. My arrest in Sai Baba's ashram and the bus crash on the way to Ooty had shaken me up. Getting lost in the temple at Madurai and the road accident at Auroville had shown me my vulnerability. The experience in the Matrimandir had left me questioning my very sense of self, while the brief affair with Lars had reminded me of my need, and capacity, for love and affection.

In the story of the Buddha, there is an episode known as the "Four Sights". Against his father's wishes, the young prince Gotama leaves the luxury and security of the palace to experience the real world. As he travels, he sees an old man, a sick man, a dead man, and finally a peaceful-looking monk. The first three sights reveal those aspects of life from which his life have so far shielded him. The fourth shows him the possibility of a new way to approach earthly existence.

In my own way, I had left the palace of modern life in the West. Through my own illness and injuries, I too had glimpsed the fragility of the body and the precariousness of life. And finally, I had met people who were living with love and faith and expressing their spirituality through kindness, devotion and community.

There are differences between cultures and countries that are hard to define and pin down in words. Climate and culture, language and landscape, are just some of the more obvious elements that make places feel different. Beneath these are subtleties almost impossible to define. How do you articulate a sense of time flowing differently? Or of events unfolding in other, more mysterious ways?

A sense of the sacred. It is hard to avoid clichés when invoking the spirit of India, but that is the closest I can come to summing up what I found on my journey. Living with this sense – if only for a while – had changed me, and my heart had finally opened.

The Author

Jon Stein is a writer and musician based in Totnes, Devon. He draws his inspiration from nature, spirituality and community. He is a keen traveller and spends his winters abroad – mostly in Andalucia, Spain – where he hopes to base his next book.

Fairway Publishing

In 1926, Joseph Stein, a Jewish immigrant with a young family, set up as a printer in the East End of London. The business began with a single foot-treadle propelled machine in the couple's bedroom. Later, the company was renamed the Fairway Press – a name chosen to reflect Joseph's intention to deal with his clients 'in a fair way'.

In 1939, Joseph finally achieved his ambition of becoming a City Printer — that is, having his firm based in the City of London — only to witness its complete destruction in the Blitz.

After the War, the Stein family relocated to Reading where Joseph and his son, Jack, relaunched the Fairway Press. The company grew through several changes of premises until 1971, when a factory was found in Silver Street. Here, Jack Stein oversaw the further development of the business until his retirement in 1993.

In 2012, Jon Stein decided to carry on the name of Fairway — this time in the context of publishing, rather than printing.

An environmentally friendly book printed and bound in England by
www.printondemand-worldwide.com

This book is made entirely of chain-of-custody materials